Golf
in
Georgia

Tom McCollister

LONGSTREET PRESS
Atlanta, Georgia

Published by LONGSTREET PRESS, INC.
a subsidiary of Cox Newspapers,
a division of Cox Enterprises, Inc.
2140 Newmarket Parkway
Suite 118
Marietta, Georgia 30067

Copyright © 1992 by Tom McCollister

Printed in the United States of America

1st printing, 1993

Library of Congress Catalog Number 92-84009

ISBN: 1-56352-075-3

This book was printed by R. R. Donnelley & Sons, Harrisonburg, VA.

Cover design by Jill Dible
Book design by Laura McDonald

CONTENTS

ACKNOWLEDGMENTS

John Byrwa
Georgia State Golf Association

INTRODUCTION

This is your guide to golf in Georgia, a comprehensive look at the state's almost 300 courses — public, private, semi-private and resort. There's no other book like it.

In these pages, we tell you where the courses are; how to contact the pro shops; what it costs to play; whether you can walk; the yardage from the tips and from the front; the course ratings from those markers as it relates to par, and whether it's nine, 18 or more holes. In some cases, we have offered comments and anecdotes on many of the courses.

There is tremendous variety in the state's courses, from the mountains to the seashore, and most of them are open to the public. The listed green and cart fees are based on current information supplied to us by the club's staff, but like the price of anything else, they are subject to change. And it's always wise to call ahead for reservations and dress codes.

Though the private clubs generally are for members only, some clubs have reciprocal arrangements with other clubs in the state, and your local professional can arrange playing privileges.

Golf in Georgia is more than a listing, however. It is a history book offering insights to some of the state's most famous clubs. You will find the mark of the great Bobby Jones not only on Augusta National, home of the Masters, but also at East Lake, the Atlanta Athletic Club, Capital City Club and Peachtree Golf Club.

Jones, who won golf's grand slam in 1930, was not only a great player but recognized talent in others as well. He arranged a membership at Atlanta's East Lake Golf Club for young Tommy Barnes in the early 1930s, and in 1989 Barnes shot 62 to break Jones' venerable course record of 63.

You will read of The Savannah Golf Club, the oldest club in the U.S.; Idle Hour in Macon that once was a horse track; how the Atlanta Country Club was conceived to host a PGA Tour event; and of the three major championships held at the Athletic Club.

We hope you enjoy **Golf in Georgia**.

Golf
in
Georgia

The Islands of Lake Lanier

North Georgia

ARROWHEAD COUNTRY CLUB

Jasper (706) 692-5634   9 holes, Par 72, Private
Opened: 1967   *Architect:* George Rice

Yardage:	Blue tees — 3,270
	Women's tees — 2,280
Course Rating:	Blues — 71.7
	Women's — 73.2

BATTLEFIELD GOLF CLUB

Ft. Oglethorpe (706) 866-1363   18 holes, Par 72, Private
Opened: 1972   *Architect:* Harry Shoemaker

Yardage:	Blue tees — 6,689
	Women's tees — 5,994
Course Rating:	Blues — 71.8
	Women's — 70.7

BEKAERT EMPLOYEES ATHLETIC ASSOCIATION

Lindale (706) 234-8010   9 holes, Par 72, Semi-Private
Opened: 1963   *Architect:* Bob McGee

Greens Fee:	$15.50 with cart daily; $25.50 weekends, holidays. Walking allowed.
Yardage:	Blue tees — 6,022
	Women's tees — 5,090
Course Rating:	Blues — 68.3
	Women's — Not rated

BENT TREE COUNTRY CLUB

Jasper (706) 893-2626   18 holes, Par 72, Private
Opened: 1973   *Architect:* Joe Lee

Yardage:	Blue tees — 6,587
	Women's tees — 4,895
Course Rating:	Blues — 71.7
	Women's — 70.2

BUTTERNUT CREEK GOLF CLUB

Blairsville (706) 745-5153   18 holes, Par 72, Public
Opened: 1952   *Architect:* Bill Watts

Greens Fee:	To be determined when second nine opens later this spring.
Yardage:	Championship tees — 6,505
	Blue tees — 6,110
	Women's tee — 5,280
Course Rating:	Championship — Not rated
	Blues — 68.3
	Women's — 69.1

CALLIER SPRINGS COUNTRY CLUB

Rome (404) 234-1691   9 holes, Par 70, Semi-Private
Opened: 1939   *Architect:* Unknown

Greens Fee:	$18 with cart daily; $23 weekends, holidays. Walking allowed.
Yardage:	Blue tees — 2,869
	Women's tees — 2,469
Course Rating:	Blues — 67.8
	Women's — 66.2

CANTON GOLF CLUB

Canton (706) 479-2772   9 holes, Par 71, Private
Opened: 1936   *Architect:* Unknown

Yardage: Blue tees — 6,198
                         Women's tees — 5,470
Course Rating: Blues — 69.3
                         Women's — 68.2

CARTERSVILLE COUNTRY CLUB

Cartersville (706) 382-1611   18 holes, Par 72, Private
Opened: 1954   *Architect:* Unknown

Yardage: Blue tees — 6,672
                         Women's tees — 5,556
Course Rating: Blues — 72.5
                         Women's — 71.5

CHATEAU ELAN GOLF CLUB

Braselton (404) 339-9838   18 holes, Par 72, Public
Opened: 1989   *Architect:* Denis Griffiths

Green Fees: $50 with cart. Walking allowed on
                         weekdays.

Yardage: Championship tees — 7,030
                         Blue tees — 6,484
                         Women's tees — 5,092
Course Rating: Championship — 73.5
                         Blues — 71.1
                         Women's — 70.8

Comment: Though no vote has been taken, this Denis Griffiths-designed course rates as the finest daily fee course in the state. There are 16 excellent holes — No. 2 is awful and the 17th is close to it — and you have to golf your ball to score well. Water comes into play on eight holes and there are 87 bunkers, but many of them define the holes rather than intimidate the player. Also, there is no finer practice facility anywhere.

Every hole is a challenge at Chateau Elan.

CHATTAHOOCHEE GOLF CLUB

Gainesville (706) 532-0066   18 holes, Par 72, Public
Opened: 1956   *Architect:* Robert Trent Jones

Greens Fee: $35 with cart. Walking allowed.

Yardage: Blue tees — 6,900
           Women's tees — 4,980
Course Rating: Blues — 72.1
           Women's — 64.5

Comment: This is where 1973 Masters champion Tommy Aaron cut his teeth, as well as Tommy Valentine, who played the PGA Tour for several years. The course is set in the rolling foothills of north Georgia and has the reputation — well deserved — of having some of the largest, fastest greens in the state. The par 4s are rather short, but tight, and the par 5s are long and wide.

CHEROKEE GOLF AND COUNTRY CLUB

Cedartown (706) 748-2800	18 holes, Par 72, Private
Opened: 1961	*Architect:* Members

Yardage:	Blue tees — 6,719
	Women's tees — 5,287
Course Rating:	Blues — 71.9
	Women's — 69.9

CHICOPEE WOODS GOLF COURSE

Gainesville (706) 534-7322	18 holes, Par 72, Public
Opened: 1991	*Architect:* Denis Griffiths

Greens fee:	$36.75 with cart. Walking allowed.

Yardage:	Championship tees — 7,040
	Blue tees — 6,606
	Women's tees — 5,001
Course Rating:	Championship — 74.1
	Blue — 72.1
	Women's — 69.0

Comment: Whoa, Nellie, as Keith Jackson would say. A look at the course rating tells it all. There are some great holes, demanding high, long tee shots. Don't hit any ground balls here. The mid to low handicapper will love it. The high handicapper, however, won't have much fun.

COOSA COUNTRY CLUB

Rome (706) 234-2200	18 holes, Par 72, Private
Opened: 1908	*Architect:* George Cobb

Yardage:	Blue tees — 6,786
	Women's tees — 5,429
Course Rating:	Blues — 71.9
	Women's — 70.7

COUNTRY LAND GOLF COURSE

Cumming (706) 887-0006	18 holes, Par 70, Semi-Private
Opened: 1991	*Architect:* Mike Young
Greens fee:	$26 with cart daily; $29 weekends, holidays. Walking allowed weekdays.
Yardage:	Blue tees — 6,050
	Women's tees — 4,200
Course Rating:	Blues — 68.5
	Women's (Par 69) — 66.6

Comment: Don't let the yardage lull you into thinking "no problem." You have to play around here. It's short, but tight, and if you don't hit your irons good, the old handicap will take a beating.

DALTON GOLF & COUNTRY CLUB

Dalton (706) 259-8547	18 holes, Par 72, Private
Opened: 1924	*Architects:* Kirby/Player
Yardage:	Championship tees — 6,674
	Blue tees — 6,213
	Women's tees — 5,117
Course Rating:	Championship — 71.8
	Blue — 69.6
	Women's — 70.4

DEER TRAIL COUNTRY CLUB

Commerce (706) 335-3987	9 holes, Par 36, Semi-Private
Opened: 1946	*Architect:* Unknown
Greens Fee:	$16 with cart daily; $18 weekends, holidays. Walking allowed.
Yardage:	Blue tees — 3,003
	Women's tees — Same
Course Rating:	Blues — 68.1
	Women's — Not rated

THE FARM GOLF CLUB

Rocky Face (706) 673-4546   18 holes, Par 72, Private
Opened: 1988   *Architect:* Tom Fazio

Yardage:	Championship tees — 6,896
	Blue tees — 6,394
	Women's tees — 5,338
Course Rating:	Championship — 73.9
	Blues — 71.6
	Women's — 71.4

FIELDS FERRY GOLF CLUB

Calhoun (706) 625-5666   18 holes, Par 72, Public
Opened: 1992   *Architect:* Arthur Davis

Greens fee: $25 with cart daily; $30 weekends, holidays. Walking allowed weekdays.

Yardage: Blue tees — 6,587
                   Women's tees — 5,355
Course Rating: To be rated in spring

Comment: It has a Scottish feeling at the start, then segues into rolling hills with beautiful mountain views. There is one par 5 with an island green. The tees are big enough to let you pick your own comfort zone. The course just opened, but looks like it's been there for awhile.

A rustic touch at Fields Ferry in Calhoun

HARTWELL GOLF CLUB

Hartwell (706) 376-8161   18 holes, Par 71, Semi-Private
Opened: 1914   *Architect:* Members

Greens Fee: $22.05 with cart daily; $24.25 weekends,
holidays. Walking allowed weekdays.

Yardage: Blue tees — 5,987
Women's tees — 4,598
Course Rating: Blues — 70.3
Women's — 68.3

HORSELEG CREEK COUNTRY CLUB

Rome (706) 291-2406   18 holes, Par 72, Private
Opened: 1958   *Architect:* Unknown

Yardage: Blue tees — 6,507
Women's tees — 5,221
Course Rating: Blues — 70.5
Women's — 67.7

INNSBRUCK GOLF CLUB

Helen (706) 878-2100   18 holes, Par 72, Public
Opened: 1987   *Architect:* Bill Watts

Greens fee: $26 with cart daily; $36 weekends, holidays.
No walking.

Yardage: Blue tees — 6,748
Women's tees — 5,174
Course Rating: Blues — 72.4
Women's — 69.9

Comment: A true mountain course, but curiously enough, there's plenty of room to play and every shot isn't up hill. The 18th may be one of the toughest par 4s around. This course is operated by American Golf Corp., which also leases the City of Atlanta courses.

KRAFTSMEN'S CLUB

Rome (706) 235-9377   9 holes, Par 72, Public
Opened: 1963   *Architect:* Unknown

Greens fee: $19 with cart daily; $22 weekends, holidays.
Walking allowed.

Yardage: Blue tees — 5,659
Women's tees — 5,220
Course Rating: Blues — 67.9
Women's — 70.0

LAKE ARROWHEAD RESORT & COUNTRY CLUB

Waleska (706) 479-5505   18 holes, Par 72, Semi-Private
Opened: 1973   *Architect:* Unknown

Greens fee: $30 with cart daily; $38 weekends, holidays.
Walking allowed at non-peak times.

Yardage: Blue tees — 6,400
Women's tees — 4,468
Course Rating: Blues — 71.2
Women's — 66.3

LAKE LANIER ISLANDS HILTON RESORT

Lake Lanier Islands (404) 945-8787   18 holes, Par 72, Public
Opened: 1989   *Architects:* Joe Lee/Rocky Roquemore

Greens fee: $39 with cart daily; $45 weekends, holidays.
(Nov. 1-Mar. 1) $35 every day. No walking.

Yardage: Championship tees — 6,341
Blue tees — 6,104
Women's tees — 4,935
Course Rating: Championship — 70.1
Blues — 68.6
Women's — 68.3

Comment: Don't bring your hooks, slices, tops and pop-ups

here. The lake will get them. It's fun, though — a shot-maker's delight. You can bite off all you can chew on several holes where the lake comes into play, but overall, accuracy will serve you better than brute strength. Good greens with subtle breaks.

MEADOW LAKES GOLF COURSE

Cedartown (706) 748-4942   18 holes, Par 72, Semi-Private
Opened: 1987   *Architect:* Ken Scodecek

Greens fee:	$25.50 with cart daily; $32 weekends, holidays. Walking allowed.
Yardage:	Blue tees — 6,509
	Women's tees — 5,255
Course Rating:	Blues — 71.8
	Women's — 70.8

NOB NORTH GOLF COURSE

Cohutta (706) 694-8505   18 holes, Par 72, Public
Opened: 1978   *Architect:* Kirby Player

Greens fee:	$26 with cart. Walking allowed.
Yardage:	Blue tees — 6,500
	Women's tees — 6,100
Course Rating:	Blues — 71.7
	Women's — 71.7

Comment: Before the influx of upscale daily fee courses in the Atlanta area, Nob North just a bit north of Dalton was the place to go, and still is for many golfers. It's that good and worth the drive. There are no weak holes, it is well-bunkered, and has tremendous greens — though they are a bit severe in both undulation and speed. Try it, you'll like it.

THE ORCHARD GOLF AND COUNTRY CLUB

Turnerville (706) 754-3156   18 holes, Par 72, Private
Opened: 1991   *Architect:* Dan Maples

Yardage: Championship tees — 6,925
                     Blue tees — 6,278
                     Women's tees — 4,838
Course Rating: Championship — 73.3
                     Blues — 70.4
                     Women's — 68.4

PAULDING COUNTRY CLUB

Dallas (404) 445-7655   9 holes, Par 72, Public
Opened: 1960   *Architect:* Bobby Jones

Greens fee: $20 with cart daily; $25 weekends, holidays.
                     Walking allowed.

Yardage: Blue tees — 3,240
Course Rating: Blues — Not rated

PINE LAKES GOLF & COUNTRY CLUB

Chatsworth (706) 695-9300   18 holes, Par 71, Semi-Private
Opened: 1963   *Architect:* Unknown

Greens Fee: $12 with cart daily; $22 weekends, holidays.
                     Walking allowed after 2 p.m.

Yardage: Blue tees — 6,300
                     Women's tees — 5,200
Course Rating: Blues — 69.8
                     Women's — 70.1

PROSPECT VALLEY GOLF CLUB

Rockmart (706) 684-5961   9 holes, Par 72, Public
Opened: 1970   *Architect:* Frank Herring

Greens fee: $16 with cart. Walking allowed.

Yardage: Blue tees — 3,100
Course Rating: Blues — 67.1

RABUN COUNTY GOLF CLUB

Clayton (706) 782-5500   9 holes, Par 70, Public
Opened: 1940   *Architect:* Work Projects Adm.

Greens fee: $18 with cart. Walking allowed.

Yardage: Blue tees — 5,322
                    Women's tees — 4,311
Course Rating: Blues — 65.7
                    Women's — 64.0

RIDGE VALLEY GOLF COURSE

Adairsville (706) 291-9049   9 holes, Par 37, Public
Opened: 1988   *Architect:* Unknown

Greens fee: $13.65 with cart. Walking allowed.

Yardage: Blue tees — 3,167
                    Women's tees — 2,865
Course Rating: Blues — 71.0
                    Women's — 75.9

ROYAL LAKES GOLF & COUNTRY CLUB

Flowery Branch (706) 535-8800   18 holes, Par 72, Semi-Private
Opened: 1989   *Architect:* Arthur Davis

Greens fee: $38 with cart daily; $40 weekends, holidays.
                    Walking allowed weekdays.

Yardage:	Blue tees — 6,871
	Women's tees — 5,325
Course Rating:	Blues — 72.5
	Women's — 70.3

Comment: Don't be discouraged if your first round here isn't a good one. It takes some getting used to, but is worth a second trip. You have to know where to hit it, and once you do you'll like it. And if you like fast, undulating greens, they've got 18 of them here.

ROYAL OAKS GOLF CLUB

Cartersville (706) 382-3999   18 holes, Par 72, Public
Opened: 1979   *Architects:* Arthur Davis/David Bingman

Greens fee: $28 with cart daily; $30 weekends, holidays. Walking allowed.

Yardage: Blue tees — 6,420
     Women's tees — 4,890
Course Rating: Blues — 70.0
     Women's — 71.0

SCONTI GOLF CLUB

Big Canoe (404) 268-5103   27 holes, Par 72, Semi-Private
Opened: Creek, Choctaw 1972   *Architect:* Joe Lee
     Cherokee 1992

CHOCTAW/CHEROKEE

Yardage: Blue tees — 6,371
     Women's tees — 4,933
Course Rating: Blues — 71.0
     Women's — 68.6

CREEK/CHOCTAW

Yardage: Blue tees — 6,276
     Women's tees — 5,159
Course Rating: Blues — 70.2
     Women's — 70.1

CHEROKEE/CREEK

Yardage:	Blue tees — 6,247
	Women's tees — 4,818
Course Rating:	Blues — 70.4
	Women's — 68.1

SKITT MOUNTAIN GOLF COURSE

Cleveland (706) 865-2277   18 holes, Par 70, Public
Opened: 1969   *Architect:* Unknown

Greens fee:	$20 with cart daily; $24 weekends, holidays. Walking allowed.
Yardage:	Blue tees — 6,020
	Women's tees — 4,584
Course Rating:	Blues — 68.5
	Women's — 65.9

SKY VALLEY RESORT

Dillard (706) 746-5303   18 holes, Par 72, Public
Opened: 1972   *Architects:* Larry McClure/Bill Watts

Greens fee:	$34 with cart daily; $39 weekends, holidays. Walking allowed after 2 p.m.
Yardage:	Blue tees — 6,388
	Women's tees — 5,066
Course Rating:	Blues — 72.1
	Women's — 69.9

Comment: This sporty track is at 3,500 feet elevation. It's under new ownership, and is the only course in Georgia with bent-grass fairways. Plus, the greens are perfect.

Scenic vistas of North Georgia's Sky Valley

STOUFFER PINE ISLE RESORT

Lake Lanier Island (404) 945-8921   18 holes, Par 72, Public
Opened: 1975   *Architects:* Ron Kirby/Gary Player

Greens fee: $56.70 with cart daily; $67.20 weekends,
                       holidays. Walking allowed after 4 p.m.

Yardage: Blue tees — 6,500
                       Women's tees — 5,297
Course Rating: Blues — 71.4
                       Women's — 70.5

Comment: The course rating is a joke. It's much tougher. It's up one hill and down another, and Lake Lanier comes into play on seven holes. No. 5 is one of those hold-your-breath-until-it-lands tees, because it has to cross a finger of the lake. The closing holes, 15-18, are tremendous. The LPGA's World Championship of Women's Golf made this home during the mid to late 80s. Not a good place for those who can't break 100.

TOCCOA GOLF & COUNTRY CLUB

Toccoa (706) 886-6545   9 holes, Par 72, Semi-Private
Opened: 1941   *Architect:* Unknown

Greens fee:	$19 with cart daily; $22 weekends, holidays. Walking allowed.
Yardage:	Blue tees — 5,922 Women's tees — 4,957
Course Rating:	Blues — 68.5 Women's — 68.8

TRION GOLF COURSE

Trion (706) 734-2712   9 holes, Par 72, Semi-Private
Opened: 1932   *Architect:* Unknown

Greens Fee:	$16 with cart daily; $18 weekends, holidays. Walking allowed.
Yardage:	Blue tees — 2,972 Women's tees — 2,572
Course Rating:	Blues — 67.0 Women's — 56.0

WHITEPATH GOLF COURSE

Ellijay (706) 276-3080   18 holes, Par 72, Public
Opened: 1984   *Architect:* Rocky Roquemore

Greens fee:	$22 with cart daily; $25 weekends, holidays. No walking.
Yardage:	Blue tees — 6,172 Women's tees — 5,298
Course Rating:	Blues — 68.9 Women's — 67.4

Metro Atlanta

ALFRED TUP HOLMES CLUB

Atlanta (404) 753-6158   18 holes, Par 72, Public
Opened: 1920   *Architect:* Unknown

Greens Fee:	$24.38 with cart daily; $26.50 weekends, holidays. Walking allowed.
Yardage:	Blue tees — 6,159
	Women's tees — 5,124
Course Rating:	Blues — 69.7
	Women's — 69.2

Comment: Another City of Atlanta course that has undergone many changes, all for the better. It sits on the site of the Confederate breastworks that protected the city during the Battle of Atlanta. There are too many doglegs and blind shots.

ANSLEY GOLF CLUB

Atlanta (404) 897-7717   9 holes, Par 72, Private
Opened: 1912   *Architect:* Unknown

Yardage:	Championship tees — 6,800
	Blue tees — 6,308
	Women's tees — 5,248
Course Rating:	Championship — 72.9
	Blues — 70.6
	Women's — 65.8

The 15th at Atlanta Athletic Club's Highlands Course

ATLANTA ATHLETIC CLUB

While much of Atlanta Athletic Club's rich history is tied to its former digs at East Lake on Alston Avenue near Decatur, the "new bunch," as some old-time East Lakers refer to them, has carried on the spirit of golfing excellence.

The AAC was, after all, Bob Jones' club, and you don't treat such a legacy lightly. And while it hasn't produced another player of Jones calibre — few have — it is carrying on the tradition.

Those years at East Lake will remain distinctive due to a number of outstanding champions, and AAC continues to be home to national champions who have groomed their games on two world class courses — Highlands and Riverside.

From green to tee on Highlands 17th

Martha Kirouac won the 1970 U.S. Women's Amateur, made the winning putt for the U.S. in the 1970 Women's World Amateur Team Championship and won the 1990 Women's Southern Amateur.

Tom Forkner was ranked among the top 10 amateurs in 1974 and won the Western Seniors Championship in 1978, '80, '83 and '86. Buck Hightower was International Seniors champion in '76, won the '79 American Seniors Championship in '79, and won the American Match Play title in '86 at the age of 69.

Perhaps AAC's greatest contribution to this city's golf scene is the strong role it has played in bringing major golf events to the area. AAC members proudly boast of being one of the few clubs, maybe the only one, to host a major tournament in each of the past five decades.

The U.S. Women's Amateur was held at East Lake in 1950, as well as the 1963 Ryder Cup, and, since moving, the 1976 U.S. Open, won by Jerry Pate. The 1981 PGA Championship, where hometown boy Larry Nelson won his first major title; the Junior World Cup in '82; the Mid-

JERRY PATE
5 IRON SHOT ON 72ND HOLE
194 YARDS
U.S. OPEN CHAMPIONSHIP
JUNE 20,1976

Remembering Jerry Pate's 5-iron shot to the 18th green in the 1976 U.S. Open at Atlanta Athletic Club

Amateur Championship in '84 and the U.S. Women's Open in '90 were all held at East Lake.

More could be on the way. The club has invited the United States Golf Association to play its 1998 U.S. Open here, and a decision is expected early next year.

In preserving the history of the club and its most famous member, in 1976 the Athletic Club dedicated the Bob Jones Room. While Jones was not interested in a memorial to himself, he was interested in preserving the record of all who had made contributions to the Athletic Club.

While the room is dominated by Bob Jones, the honorees include outstanding past presidents, the great golfers who played out of the AAC and its past club professionals — the Sargents — George, Jack and Harold.

Included in the Jones room are the trophies from his Grand Slam year, rare books, photographs, personal letters, vintage golf clubs and balls, and a statuette of Jones in his classic swing.

ATLANTA ATHLETIC CLUB

Duluth (404) 448-8552   36 holes, Both par 72, Private

HIGHLANDS
Opened: 1965   *Architects:* Robert Trent Jones/Joe Finger

Yardage: Championship tees — 7,148
                   Blue tees — 6,833
                   Women's tees — 5,406
Course Rating: Championship — 74.8
                   Blues — 73.3
                   Women's — 73.0

RIVERSIDE

Opened: 1967   *Architect:* Robert Trent Jones

Yardage: Championship tees — 6,958
                           Blue tees — 6,695
                           Women's tees — 5,497
Course Rating: Championship — 73.6
                           Blues — 72.4
                           Women's — 73.1

ATLANTA COUNTRY CLUB

In most cases, the idea behind the development of a country club is to provide a social and recreational atmosphere for its members. But from the minute the late Jim Clay began putting together the group that would establish the Atlanta Country Club, the focus was to bring a PGA Tour event to Atlanta.

Groundbreaking for the Atlanta Country Club came in 1963, the course opened in 1965, and on Oct. 1, 1967, New Zealand's Bob Charles won the first Atlanta Classic. The purse was only $110,000, and Charles' winning share was $22,000.

From that humble beginning, the Classic has grown into one of the most successful stops on the Tour, and the men who play here each spring consider the Willard Byrd-designed course demanding, yet fair. The tournament has been held each year with the exception of 1976 when officials graciously stepped aside, as the area put all its efforts into making the U.S. Open a success at the Atlanta Athletic Club's Highlands course.

The course has been altered through the years. Jack Nicklaus redesigned the signature 13th hole, making it one of the most scenic par 3s on the tour.

The list of winners there is impressive. Nicklaus won the Classic in 1973 and again in '74, when ACC had the honor

Driving off No.1 at Atlanta Country Club's BellSouth Classic

of hosting the first Tournament Players Championship. Home-grown Larry Nelson has taken the title twice, as has Hale Irwin, Tom Kite and Wayne Levi.

Gainesville's Tommy Aaron made the Classic his first official PGA Tour victory. Tommy Valentine, another Gainesville native, came close in 1981, but lost on the third hole of sudden death to Tom Watson, who earlier that year won his second Masters.

ATLANTA COUNTRY CLUB

Marietta (404) 953-1211	18 holes, Par 72, Private
Opened: 1965	*Architect:* Willard Byrd

Yardage:	Championship tees — 7,018
	Blue tees — 6,452
	Women's tees — 5,323
Course Rating:	Championship — 74.3
	Blues — 71.6
	Women's — 71.0

ATLANTA NATIONAL GOLF CLUB

Alpharetta (404) 442-8802   18 holes, Par 72, Private
Opened: 1988   *Architects:* Pete Dye/P.B. Dye

Yardage:	Championship tees — 7,009
	Blue tees — 6,540
	Women's tees — 4,681
Course Rating:	Championship — 74.6
	Blues — 72.4
	Women's — 68.5

BERKELEY HILLS COUNTRY CLUB

Duluth (404) 448-4661   27 holes, Private
Opened: 1964   *Architect:* Gary Player

KING HILLS/PINE HILLS

Yardage:	Blue tees — 6,561
	Women's tees — 5,472
Course Rating:	Blues — 72.0
	Women's — 72.0

PINE HILLS/ROLLING HILLS

Yardage:	Blue tees — 6,338
	Women's tees — 5,408
Course Rating:	Blues — 71.0
	Women's — 71.6

ROLLING HILLS/KING HILLS

Yardage:	Blue tees — 6,399
	Women's tees — 5,514
Course Rating:	Blues — 71.5
	Women's — 71.6

Up the hill to the 12th at Bobby Jones Course

BOBBY JONES GOLF COURSE

Atlanta (404) 355-1009   18 holes, Par 71, Public
Opened: 1934   *Architect:* Unknown

Greens Fee: $25.38 with cart daily; $28 weekends,
                        holidays. Walking allowed.

Yardage: Blue tees — 6,155
                        Women's tees — 4,661
Course Rating: Blues — 69.0
                        Women's — 67.6

Comment: A lot of people have learned to play golf at Bobby Jones. They've put up with horrible fairways and greens, but keep coming back. It's like a mismatched set of clubs and x-out golf balls — not very pretty — but as comfortable as an old pair of slippers.

BRAELINN GOLF CLUB

Peachtree City (404) 631-3100   18 holes, Par 72, Private
Opened: 1989   *Architect:* Joe Lee

Yardage:	Championship tees — 6,815
	Blue tees — 6,390
	Women's tees — 5,275
Course Rating:	Championship — 72.9
	Blues — 71.0
	Women's — 70.5

BROOKFIELD COUNTRY CLUB

Roswell (404) 992-9230   18 holes, Par 72, Private
Opened: 1972   *Architects:* Randy Nichols/Howard Chatham

Yardage:	Blue tees — 6,535
	Women's — 5,394
Course Rating:	Blues — 71.4
	Women's — 71.9

BROOKSTONE GOLF & COUNTRY CLUB

Acworth (404) 425-8500   18 holes, Par 72, Private
Opened: 1988   *Architect:* Larry Nelson

Yardage:	Championship tees — 6,815
	Blue tees — 6,409
	Women's tees — 5,941
Course Rating:	Championship — 73.0
	Blues — 71.1
	Women's — 68.3

BROWNS MILL GOLF COURSE

Atlanta (404) 366-3573 18 holes, Par 72, Public
Opened: 1970 *Architect:* Unknown

Greens Fee: $26 with cart daily; $29 weekends, holidays. Walking allowed.

Yardage: Blue tees — 6,600
Women's tees — 5,600

Course Rating: Blues — 71.0
Women's — 71.4

Comment: Considering the factors of playability, layout and pace of play, Browns Mill is the best of the four City of Atlanta courses now under lease to American Golf Corporation. The low handicapper will find it a comfort to his soul and the beginner won't need a dozen balls to make it around. The 448-yard, par 4 12th is one the toughest pars in town.

CANONGATE GOLF CLUB I

Palmetto (404) 463-3342 18 holes, Par 72, Private
Opened: 1964 *Architects:* Joe Lee/Dick Wilson

Yardage: Blue tees — 6,834
Women's tees — 6,100

Course Rating: Blues — 72.0
Women's — 70.5

CANTERBURY GOLF CLUB

Marietta (404) 926-3702 18 holes, Par 71, Private
Opened: 1968 *Architect:* Unknown

Yardage: Blue tees — 6,203
Women's tees — 5,000

Course Rating: Blues — 70.1
Women's — 70.5

CAPITAL CITY CLUB

Capital City Club was a downtown businessman's club and gathering place for the rich and famous in its early days. But once it leased the old Brookhaven Country Club in 1911 and purchased it in 1915, it became the hotbed of Atlanta's golfing elite.

The first Georgia State Amateur was held at Capital City Club in 1916, and 14-year-old Bobby Jones won the contest, beating his close friend Perry Adair 2 and 1 in the final. It also hosted the 1926, '32, '36 and '46 Amateurs.

The great British pair of Ted Ray and Harry Vardon played an exhibition match there in 1913.

Capital City Club also holds a place in the PGA Tour record book. In 1945, Byron Nelson won 11 consecutive tournaments. No. 5 came in the Atlanta Open, where he shot 21-under and received a check for $2,000. The tournament was held April 5-8, normally the dates for the Masters, which was not played that year due to wartime restrictions.

Women golfers also played a major role in Capital City's history. The first Ladies Invitational was held in 1923, won by Dot Kirby, a club member. The Women's Western Open, which hadn't been held in the South since 1913, was played at Capital City in 1947. The great Louis Suggs defeated Kirby.

While the Capital City Club had, and continues to have, many of the Atlanta area's most powerful men, and now women, as members, it wasn't without a character or two to liven things up. One of those members was the late Bobby Dodd, who joined in 1934 after coming to Georgia Tech as an assistant coach. Dodd was a riverboat gambler at heart and wagering on the golf course was almost a passion. Bets of $100 or more were common. He and his friends often played until after dark, stationing club caddies to watch for their shots. Once on the green, they would set newspapers on fire in order to see the hole.

CAPITAL CITY CLUB

Atlanta (404) 233-2121   18 holes, Par 72, Private
Opened: 1911   *Architect:* Redesigned several times

Yardage:	Blue tees — 6,370
	Women's tees — 5,220
Course Rating:	Blues — 70.9
	Women's — 70.6

Centennial's 18th green and clubhouse

CENTENNIAL GOLF CLUB

Acworth (404) 975-1000	18 holes, Par 72, Public
Opened: 1990	*Architect:* Larry Nelson

Green Fees:	$32.35 daily with cart; $42.50 weekends, holidays. Walking allowed at times.
Yardage:	Championship tees — 6,850
	Blue tees — 6,350
	Women's tees — 5,109
Course Rating:	Championship — 73.1
	Blues — 70.8
	Women's — 69.5

Comment: Nelson throws every challenge in the game your way on this rolling piece of property. You have to drive it strongly, hit your irons good and you'd better bring your A- putting game. The front side is a stroke or three easier than the back, which ends with a tough par 3 and an even tougher par 4.

CHAMPIONS AT RIVER'S EDGE

Fayetteville (404) 460-1098	18 holes, Par 71, Public
Opened: 1989	*Architect:* Bobby Weed

Greens fee:	$28 with cart daily; $36 weekends, holidays. No walking.
Yardage:	Blue tees — 6,292
	Women's tees — 4,842
Course Rating:	Blues — 70.8
	Women's — 64.4

Comment: Long and strong. This course has some of the best designed greens you'll find anywhere. Part of the course winds through the valley of the Flint River. Tight in spots, wide open in others, River's Edge gives you a pretty good idea of what shape your game is in.

The 8th at Champions of Atlanta demands accuracy.

CHAMPIONS CLUB OF ATLANTA

Alpharetta (404) 343-9700   18 holes, Par 72, Semi-Private
Opened: 1991   *Architects:* D.J. DeVictor/Steve Melnyk

Greens fee: $41 with cart daily; $49 weekends, holidays.
            No walking.

Yardage: Championship tees — 6,725
            Blue tees — 6,300
            Women's tees — 5,100

Course Rating: Championship — 71.5
            Blue — 68.4
            Women's — 65.7

Comment: This is a course that has improved 100 percent since it opened. You don't have to drive it long, but you better hit it straight. No. 8 is tough and 9 and 10 are three-shot par 5s. Not recommended for the beginner.

CHAPEL HILLS GOLF CLUB

Douglasville (404) 949-0030   18 holes, Par 72 Private
Opened: 1992   *Architect:* Rocky Roquemore

Yardage: Championship tees — 6,556
                   Blue tees — 6,207
                   Women's tees — 5,021
Course Rating: Championship — 70.1
                   Blues — 68.7
                   Women's — 67.3

CHEROKEE COUNTRY CLUB

Dunwoody (404) 993-4401   36 holes, Par 72s, Private

HILL COURSE
Opened: 1956   *Architect:* Willard Byrd

Yardage: Championship tees — 6,945
                   Blue tees — 6,550
                   Women's tees — 5,362
Course Rating: Championship — 73.7
                   Blues — 71.7
                   Women's — 71.7

RIVER COURSE
Opened: 1984   *Architect:* Joe Lee

Yardage: Championship tees — 6,546
                   Blue tees — 6,265
                   Women's tees — 5,018
Course Rating: Championship — 71.4
                   Blue tees — 70.0
                   Women's — 69.6

CITY CLUB MARIETTA

Marietta (404) 528-0555	18 holes, Par 71, Public
Opened: 1915	*Architect:* Redesigned in 1990 by Mike Young

Greens fee: $29 with cart daily; $39 weekends, holidays. Walking allowed.

Yardage: Blue tees — 5,900
Women's tees — 5,000

Course Rating: Blues — 67.4
Women's — 67.5

Comment: You look at the yardage and think, piece of cake. It isn't. You have to play. This was the site of the former Marietta Country Club, but it has undergone a facelift. No. 8 is a 547-yard par 5, and it's a good one.

COLLEGE PARK MUNICIPAL COURSE

College Park (404) 761-0731	9 holes, Par 36, Public
Opened: 1931	*Architect:* WPA Workforce

Greens Fee: $9.75 with cart. Walking allowed.

Yardage: Blue tees — 2,987
Women's tees — Same

Course Rating: Blues — 67.2
Women's — Not rated

COUNTRY CLUB OF THE SOUTH

Alpharetta (404) 475-6779	18 holes, Par 72, Private
Opened: 1987	*Architect:* Jack Nicklaus

Yardage: Championship tees — 6,976
Blue tees — 6,501
Women's tees — 5,164

Course Rating: Championship — 73.6
Blues — 71.8
Women's — 71.8

CROSS CREEK COUNTRY CLUB

Atlanta (404) 352-5612	18 holes, Par 54, Semi-Private
Opened: 1970	*Architect:* Unknown

Greens Fee: Nov.-Feb. $8 daily; $12 weekends, holidays. March-Oct. $12 weekdays; $16 weekends, holidays. Walking only.

Yardage: Blue tees — 1,922
Women's tees — 1,753

Course Rating: Blues — 50.0
Women's — 54.7

CUMBERLAND CREEK COUNTRY CLUB

Marietta (404) 422-3822	18 holes, Par 70, Semi-Private
Opened: 1970	*Architect:* Unknown

Greens Fee: $12 with cart daily; $16 weekends, holidays. Walking allowed.

Yardage: Blue tees — 5,400
Women's tees — 5,000

Course Rating: Blues — 67.2
Women's — Not rated

DOGWOOD GOLF & COUNTRY CLUB

Austell (404) 941-2202	18 holes, Par 72, Semi-Private
Opened: 1968	*Architect:* Unknown

Greens Fee: $25.20 daily with cart; $31.50 weekends, holidays. No walking.

Yardage: Blue tees — 6,275
Women's tees — 5,174

Course Rating: Blues — 70.5
Women's — 70.8

The 6th green at Druid Hills

DRUID HILLS

Druid Hills Golf Club has been an integral part of the Atlanta golf scene since it opened in 1914, joining the Capital City Club and Atlanta Athletic Club at East Lake.

From 1941 through 1972, Druid Hills was the site of the Dogwood Invitational Golf Tournament, one of the most prestigious events in the U.S. It was a must stop each spring for the country's top amateur players, preparing them for such national tournaments as the U.S. Amateur.

The list of winners reads like a Who's Who of golf in Georgia and the nation.

The late Gene Dahlbender Jr. of East Lake won it an amazing seven times and when he didn't, it seemed his good friend Tommy Barnes did. Barnes won four times and finished second three times.

The Dogwood's honor roll also includes two-time winner Harvie Ward Jr., who won back-to-back in 1952-'53, then took the U.S. Amateur back-to-back in '55-'56. Ward's victim in '56 was Chuck Kocsis, who four years later won the Dogwood.

The PGA Tour's Lanny Wadkins played in the Dogwood at the age of 13, invited as the national Pee Wee champion.

The Dogwood will return in 1994, again inviting the best amateurs in the country for a mid-May event.

Druid Hills has also been the host club for the State Amateur a record six times, 1920, '22, '28, '38 and '62. One of its founding members, C.V. Rainwater won in '20 and Dahlbender in '62.

DRUID HILLS GOLF CLUB

Atlanta (404) 377-1768   18 holes, Par 72, Private
Opened: 1913   *Architect:* H.H. Baker

Yardage:	Blue tees — 6,432
	Women's tees — 5,274
Course Rating:	Blues — 71.3
	Women's — 71.8

DUNWOODY COUNTRY CLUB

Dunwoody (404) 394-1928   18 holes, Par 72, Private
Opened: 1969   *Architect:* Willard Byrd

Yardage:	Championship tees — 7,007
	Blue tees — 6,508
	Women's tees — 5,333
Course Rating:	Championship — 74.0
	Blues — 71.6
	Women's — 71.4

EAGLE'S LANDING COUNTRY CLUB

Stockbridge (404) 389-9898   18 holes, Par 72, Private
Opened: 1989   *Architect:* Tom Fazio

Yardage: Championship tees — 6,986
                     Blue tees — 6,558
                     Women's tees — 5,026
Course Rating: Championship — 74.4
                     Blues — 72.4
                     Women's — 69.5

EAGLE WATCH GOLF CLUB

Woodstock (404) 591-1000   18 holes, Par 72, Public
Opened: 1989   *Architects:* Arnold Palmer/Ed Seay

Green Fees: $54.50 with cart daily, $65 weekends,
                     holidays. No walking.

Yardage: Championship tees — 6,896
                     Blue tees — 6,458
                     Women's tees — 5,243
Course Rating: Championship — 72.6
                     Blues — 70.4
                     Women's — 68.9

Comment: Eagle Watch is a huge golf course and a long-hitters delight. There are good par 4s, difficult par 3s and par 5s that offer birdie opportunities. It has a private club atmosphere from the time you drop your clubs off until you leave.

EAST LAKE

Is there a golf fan anywhere with a sense of history that the mention of Atlanta Athletic Club and its old East Lake course doesn't conjure up the memory of Robert Tyre Jones Jr.?

There shouldn't be. Even in this day of superstars galore,

Old friends Tommy Barnes (l) and Journal Sports Editor Furman Bisher celebrate Barne's record 62 at East Lake.

Jones holds a place above all others. His name is as revered in St. Andrews, Scotland as it is in Duluth, Ga., where the Atlanta Athletic Club moved its operation in 1965 after selling East Lake to some of its members who chose to remain downtown.

But it was at East Lake in 1908 that Jones began his journey to golfing immortality by winning a six-hole kids tournament, and that culminated in 1930 with the Grand Slam — victories in the U.S. and British Amateurs and U.S. and British Opens.

But Jones isn't the only great one whose roots belong to

East Lake. Long before Jones would win his first major championship, his childhood playmate and golfing companion Alexa Stirling had won three Women's Amateur titles and been runner-up twice.

Stirling was as dominating in women's golf as Jones would be in men's competition. For instance, in 1925, Stirling shot 77 to win medalist honors and become the first American woman to play 18 holes in competition with a score under 79.

East Lake's lineage didn't stop with Jones and Stirling. Instead, it inspired others. Among the men, Watts Gunn was runner-up to Jones in the 1925 Amateur and played with Jones on two Walker Cups.

Then there was Charlie Yates. He was 10 when Jones won the 1923 U.S. Open and after hearing it on the radio, he sprinted around the East Lake course spreading the news to everyone in sight. Yates, like Jones, was a Georgia Tech man. He won today's version of the NCAA championship in 1925 and three years later picked up the mantle laid down by Jones by winning the British Amateur.

There have been others whose success stopped short of national and international fame but who nevertheless kept the East Lake flame alive. Charles Harrison, Gene Dahlbender and Tommy Barnes come to mind.

And Barnes is the rest of the story.

East Lake has had no national champions in recent years, but Barnes stoked the fires of pride in 1989 when, at the age of 73, he shot a 62, breaking Jones's course record of 63 set in 1922. The irony is that in the early 1930s, it was Jones who secretly arranged an honorary membership for Barnes, who didn't discover until 25 years later who was his benefactor.

One more thing. Jones played his last round of golf on Aug. 18, 1948 at East Lake, and Barnes was in the foursome.

East Lake has survived the break-up almost 30 years ago of

the Athletic Club. And while AAC has most things material of Jones, East Lake has the memories.

EAST LAKE COUNTRY CLUB

Atlanta (404) 373-5764   18 holes, Par 72, Private
Opened: 1906   *Architect:* Donald Ross

Yardage:	Blue tees — 6,960
	Women's tees — 6,061
Course Rating:	Blues — 72.9
	Women's — 74.1

FIELDSTONE GOLF CLUB

Conyers (404) 483-4372   18 holes, Par 72, Semi-Private
Opened: 1967   *Architect:* Unknown

Greens Fee:	$25 with cart daily; $30 weekends, holidays. Walking allowed for members.
Yardage:	Blue tees — 6,458
	Women's tees — 6,100
Course Rating:	Blues — 69.9
	Women's — Not rated

FLAT CREEK GOLF CLUB

Peachtree City (404) 487-8140   27 holes, Par 72, Private

HOMESTEAD
Opened: 1968   *Architect:* Joe Lee

Yardage:	Blue tees — 3,409
	Women's tees — 2,692
Course Rating:	Blues — 36.5
	Women's — 35.2

OLD MILL

Opened: 1968		Architect: Joe Lee
Yardage:	Blue tees — 3,349	
	Women's tees — 2,607	
Course Rating:	Blues — 36.0	
	Women's — 34.5	

GRAVEYARD

Opened: 1984		Architect: Joe Lee
Yardage:	Blue tees — 3,350	
	Women's tees — 2,639	
Course Rating:	Blues — 36.1	
	Women's — 34.7	

FORT McPHERSON GOLF CLUB

Ft. McPherson (404) 752-2178   18 holes, Par 72, Military (Private)
Opened: 1929   Architect: George Cobb

Yardage:	Blue tees — 6,505
	Women's tees — 5,456
Course Rating:	Blues — 70.5
	Women's — 70.7

FOX CREEK GOLF CLUB

Smyrna (404) 435-1000   18 holes (Executive), Par 61 Public
Opened: 1985   Architect: John LaFoy

Greens Fee:	$23.10 with cart daily; $28.35 weekends, holidays. Walking allowed.
Yardage:	Blue tees — 4,018
	Women's tees — 3,065
Course Rating:	Blues — 59.6
	Women's — 57.6

It's all carry, 222 yards, to No. 6 at Golf Club of Georgia.

GOLF CLUB OF GEORGIA

Alpharetta (404) 4653
Opened: 1991

36 holes, Both par 72, Private
Architect: Arthur Hills

LAKEVIEW

Yardage:	Championship tees — 7,020
	Blue tees — 6,660
	Women's tees — 5,059
Course Rating:	Championship — 74.7
	Blues — 73.0
	Women's — 70.5

GREYSTONE GOLF CLUB

Douglasville (404) 489-9608
Opened: 1990

18 holes, Par 72, Public
Architect: Don Cottle Jr.

Greens Fee:	$25 with cart daily; $30 weekends, holidays. Walking weekdays only.
Yardage:	Blue tees — 6,106
	Women's tees — 4,522
Course Rating:	Blues — 69.0
	Women's — 65.3

HIDDEN HILLS COUNTRY CLUB

Stone Mountain (404) 981-6641   18 holes, Par 72, Private
Opened: 1972   *Architect:* Joe Lee

Yardage:	Blue tees — 6,700
	Women's tees — 5,400
Course Rating:	Blues — 72.5
	Women's — 71.2

HIGHLAND GOLF CLUB

Conyers (404) 483-4235   18 holes, Par 72, Semi-Private
Opened: 1961   *Architect:* Jack Williams

Greens Fee:	$25 with cart daily; $35 weekends, holidays. No walking.
Yardage:	Championship tees — 6,888
	Blue tees — 6,369
	Women's tees — 5,355
Course Rating:	Championship — 72.6
	Blues — 70.4
	Women's — 71.3

HONEY CREEK COUNTRY CLUB

Conyers (404) 483-6343   18 holes, Par 72, Semi-Private
Opened: 1973   *Architect:* Unknown

Greens fee:	$25.73 with cart daily; $30.98 weekends, holidays. Walking allowed weekdays and after 1 p.m. weekends, holidays.
Yardage:	Blue tees — 6,115
	Women's tees — 5,142
Course Rating:	Blues — 69.1
	Women's — 69.3

HORSESHOE BEND COUNTRY CLUB

Roswell (404) 992-2310   18 holes, Par 72, Private
Opened: 1976   *Architect:* Joe Lee

Yardage: Blue tees — 6,638
                        Women's tees — 5,355
Course Rating: Blues — 72.4
                        Women's — 71.1

INDIAN HILLS COUNTRY CLUB

Marietta (404) 971-7663   27 holes, Par 72, Private
Opened: 1970   *Architect:* Joe Lee

SEMINOLE/CHOCTAW
Yardage: Blue tees — 6,605
                        Women's tees — 5,194
Course Rating: Blues — 72.3
                        Women's — 70.6

CHOCTAW/CHEROKEE
Yardage: Blue tees — 6,565
                        Women's tees — 5,194
Course Rating: Blues — 72.0
                        Women's — 70.6

CHEROKEE/SEMINOLE
Yardage: Blue tees — 6,310
                        Women's tees — 5,209
Course Rating: Blues — 70.7
                        Women's — 70.2

LAKE SPIVEY GOLF CLUB

Jonesboro (404) 477-9836   27 holes, Par 72, Semi-Private
Opened: 1962   *Architect:* D.J. DeVictor

Greens fee: $24 with cart daily; $33 weekends, holidays. Walking allowed weekdays and after 1 p.m. weekends, holidays.

LAKESIDE/CLUBSIDE
Yardage: Blue tees — 6,750
     Women's tees — 5,318
Course Rating: Blues — 72.5
     Women's — 70.1

LAKESIDE/HILLSIDE
Yardage: Blue tees — 6,467
     Women's tees — 4,972
Course Rating: Blues — 71.4
     Women's — 68.0

HILLSIDE/CLUBSIDE
Yardage: Blue tees — 6,379
     Women's tees — 4,990
Course Rating: Blues — 70.9
     Women's — 68.3

Comment: You won't get bored playing here. Some holes are flat, some rolling. There's water and trees. And don't leave any clubs out of your bag. You will need them all. One more thing, keep all your approach shots under the hole. These greens are slick.

LAKESIDE GOLF CLUB

Atlanta (404) 344-3629   18 holes, Par 72, Public
Opened: 1962   *Architect:* George Cobb

Greens fee: $25 with cart daily; $35 weekends, holidays. No walking.

Yardage:	Blue tees — 6,603
	Women's tees — 5,417
Course Rating:	Blues — 72.2
	Women's — 71.9

Comment: Formerly a private club, Lakeside is now open to the public and located just minutes from downtown. If you like holes that dogleg, you'll love this place.

LANIER GOLF CLUB

Cumming (404) 577-1313　　　　　18 holes, Par 72, Private
Opened: 1970　　　　　　　　　　　*Architect:* Joe Lee

Yardage:	Championship tees — 6,905
	Blue tees — 6,715
	Women's tees — 5,652
Course Rating:	Championship — 66.0
	Blue — 71.1
	Women's — 70.0

THE LINKS GOLF CLUB

Jonesboro (404) 461-5100　　　　　18 holes, Par 70, Public
Opened: 1991　　　　*Architects:* Jack Gaudion Jr./Terry Anton

Greens fee:	$25 with cart daily; $29 weekends, holidays. Walking allowed after 1 p.m.
Yardage:	Blue tees — 6,376
	Women's tees — 4,398
Course Rating:	Blues — 69.4
	Women's — 64.7

Comment: It is links in name only. Though many holes are wide open and moguls are utilized, this is very much a Georgia course. It's tight, tree-lined and rolling. And it's fun. An added feature is the well-designed Wee Links, nine holes of medium yardage for the beginning junior player.

LITTLE MOUNTAIN GOLF COURSE

Ellenwood (404) 981-7921   18 holes, Par 72, Public
Opened: 1990   *Architect:* Bob Jones

Greens fee: $20 with cart daily; $25 weekends, holidays.
                      Walking allowed.

Yardage: Blue tees — 5,759
                      Women's tees — 4,892
Course Rating: Not yet rated

Comment: The classic example of no matter what the yardage indicates, you still have to hit the shots. Little Mountain isn't long, isn't easy, but it is pretty and definitely enjoyable. A new nine was added two years ago.

MARIETTA COUNTRY CLUB

Marietta (404) 426-7084   18 holes, Par 72, Private
Opened: 1990   *Architect:* Bob Cupp

Yardage: Championship tees — 6,820
                      Blue tees — 6,342
                      Women's tees — 5,133
Course Rating: Championship — 72.6
                      Blues — 70.41
                      Women's — 70.4

METROPOLITAN CLUB

Lithonia (404) 981-7696   18 holes, Par 72, Semi-Private
Opened: 1967   *Architect:* Rees Jones

Greens Fee: $32 with cart daily; $42.50 weekends,
                      holidays. Walking allowed Mon.-Thurs.

Yardage: Blue tees — 6,930
                      Women's tees — 5,966
Course Rating: Blues — 73.9
                      Women's — 75.8

Comment: No daily fee course in Atlanta has come as far as Metropolitan Club in the last 10 years. A group headed by Larry Nelson bought it in the early 80s and turned an eyesore into one of the best. From the tips, it's all you want. It's the kind of course that lulls you into a sense of false security, then breaks your heart. But it won't beat you down.

MYSTERY VALLEY GOLF COURSE

Lithonia (404) 469-6913   18 holes, Par 72, Public
Opened: 1966   *Architect:* Dick Wilson

Greens fee:	$26 with cart daily; $29 weekends, holidays. Walking allowed.
Yardage:	Blue tees — 6,705
	Women's tees — 5,815
Course Rating:	Blue — 71.5
	Women's — 72.7

Comment: The card says 6,705 yards and par of 72, but it plays longer and tougher. The par 5s won't break your back, but some of the par 4s and all the par 3s can leave you downright frustrated. The four closing holes are toughies.

NORTH FULTON GOLF COURSE

Atlanta (404) 255-0723   18 holes, Par 71, Public
Opened: 1934   *Architect:* H. Chandler Egan

Greens fee:	$25.89 with cart daily; $28 weekends, holidays. Walking allowed.
Yardage:	Blue tees — 6,570
	Women's tees — 5,120
Course Rating:	Blues — 71.8
	Women's — 69.5

Comment: It's stood the test of time and is still the best layout of all the City of Atlanta courses. If you are a good iron player, you'll score well because the greens are small. The 440-yard, par 4 18th is one of the toughest around. Slow play is a problem, however.

NORTHWOOD COUNTRY CLUB

Lawrenceville (404) 923-2991   18 holes, Par 72, Private
Opened: 1959   *Architect:* Willard Byrd

Yardage:	Blue tees — 6,853
	Women's tees — 5,630
Course Rating:	Blues — 73.1
	Women's — 72.4

THE OAKS COURSE

Covington (706) 221-0200   18 holes, Par 70, Public
Opened: 1991   *Architect:* Dick Schulz

Greens fee:	$25 with cart daily; $35 weekends, holidays. Walking allowed.
Yardage:	Blue tees — 6,420
	Women's tees — 4,634
Course Rating:	Blues — 69.5
	Women's — 64.5

Comment: You will find a nice blend of short par 4s and good par 5s. More 80 shooters are likely to hit the 70s here than on any other full-size course in the state. It's a straight forward layout, no tricks. High handicappers won't be intimidated, mid-handicappers will be rewarded and the very good player could be bored.

PEACHTREE GOLF CLUB

When Bobby Jones conceived the idea of Peachtree Golf Club, he had one thought in mind — to build a course as

much like Augusta National as possible, and better if at all possible.

Whether Jones succeeded is in the eye of the beholder, but there is general agreement that Peachtree is one of the best, and outside of Augusta National, maybe the most exclusive in Georgia.

The course, oddly enough, was built where a nursery once thrived, just as Augusta National. Robert Trent Jones, under the watchful eye of Bobby Jones, was chosen to design the course. Construction began in May of 1945, and the first nine was opened for play in 1947, the second nine in 1948.

Unlike Augusta National, however, only its members and guests can attest to its greatness. Augusta National opens its doors once a year to the masses through the Masters. Tournaments involving the outside world are not habitual at Peachtree.

In the early 1960s, Peachtree's membership granted permission for one of the Shell Wonderful World of Golf matches between Sam Snead and Julius Boros. Two days were required for the filming, and a gallery was enlisted, but spectators were requested to wear the same clothes for both days to insure serial continuity.

In 1989, the club invited the United States Golf Association and Royal and Ancient Golf Club of St. Andrews to play the 32nd Match for the Walker Cup on its course. The team from Great Britain-Ireland defeated the U.S. in this international competition, their first ever victory on American soil.

The course is magnificent, playing through tall oaks and pines. It has some of the most challenging par 4s anywhere.

One unique feature of Peachtree is its clubhouse, which Yankee Gen. William T. Sherman used as his headquarters during the Civil War. He torched much of Atlanta, but left the clubhouse standing. The grand old building still stands in its original brick coat.

PEACHTREE GOLF CLUB

Atlanta (404)233-4428   18 holes, Par 72, Private
Opened: 1948   *Architects:* Bob Jones/Robert Trent Jones

Yardage: Championship tees — 7,043
                Blue tees — 6,573
                Women's tees — 5,268
Course Rating: Championship — 74.1
                Blues — 71.8
                Women's — 71.8

PEBBLE CREEK GOLF CLUB

Jonesboro (404) 471-5455   18 holes, Par 70, Semi-Private
Opened: 1974   Architect: Unknown

Greens fee: $20.50 with cart daily; $25.50 weekends,
                holidays. Walking allowed weekdays and
                after 2 p.m. weekends, holidays.

Yardage: Blue tees — 6,015
                Women's tees — 5,326
Course Rating: Blues — 67.6
                Women's — 65.1

PINE HILLS COUNTRY CLUB

Cordele (912) 273-7587   9 holes, Par 71, Private
Opened: 1940   *Architect:* Unknown

Yardage: Blue tees — 6,134
                Women's tees — 5,652
Course Rating: Blues — 71.1
                Women's — 74.5

PINETREE COUNTRY CLUB

Kennesaw (404) 428-0553   18 holes, Par 72, Private
Opened: 1960   *Architect:* William Byrd

Yardage: Championship tees — 6,854
                    Blue tees — 6,466
                    Women's tees — 5,540
Course Rating: Championship — 72.3
                    Blues — 70.5
                    Women's — 71.6

POLO GOLF & COUNTRY CLUB

Cumming (404) 688-7656   18 holes, Par 72, Private
Opened: 1988   *Architect:* Joe Lee

Yardage: Championship tees — 6,558
                    Blue tees — 6,277
                    Women's tees — 5,788
Course Rating: Championship — 72.5
                    Blues — 71.0
                    Women's — 74.1

RIVERMONT GOLF & COUNTRY CLUB

Alpharetta (404) 993-2124   18 holes, Par 72, Private
Opened: 1974   *Architect:* Joe Lee

Yardage: Championship tees — 6,767
                    Blue tees — 6,380
                    Women's tees — 5,496
Course Rating: Championship — 72.4
                    Blue — 70.5
                    Women's — 72.0

RIVERPINES GOLF CLUB

Alpharetta (404) 442-5960   18 holes, Par 70, Public
Opened: 1992   *Architect:* Denis Griffiths

Greens fee:	$40 with cart. Walking allowed weekdays and after 1:30 weekends, holidays.
Yardage:	Championship tees — 6,511 Blue tees — 6,002 Women's tees — 4,279
Course Rating:	Not rated as of 2-1-93

Comment: There aren't many courses that satisfy the needs of both the low handicapper and the not ready for prime time players. But RiverPines does. From the tips, it's barely 6,500 yards, but good players can't take any of it for granted. And with four sets of tees, the high handicapper can find his own comfort zone. There's also a 9-hole par 3 course on the property to test your short game.

SAINT ANDREWS COUNTRY CLUB

Winston (404) 489-2200   9 holes, Par 72, Semi-Private
Opened: 1970   *Architect:* Unknown

Greens fee:	$22 with cart daily; $28 weekends, holidays. Walking allowed weekdays.
Yardage:	Blue tees — 6,620 Women's tees — 5,940
Course Rating:	Blues — 73.0 Women's — 74.0

ST. IVES COUNTRY CLUB

Duluth (404) 497-9432   18 holes, Par 72, Private
Opened: 1989   *Architect:* Tom Fazio

Yardage:	Championship tees — 6,874 Blue tees — 6,371

Course Rating:	Women's tees — 4,915
	Championship — 73.2
	Blues — 71.2
	Women's — 68.5

SETTINDOWN CREEK GOLF CLUB

Woodstock (404) 924-0635   18 holes, Par 72, Private
Opened: 1988   *Architect:* Bob Cupp

Yardage:	Championship tees — 6,960
	Blue tees — 6,507
	Women's tees — 4,965
Course Rating:	Championship — 73.6
	Blues — 71.7
	Women's — 68.7

SOUTHERNESS GOLF CLUB

Stockbridge (404) 808-6000   18 holes, Par 72, Semi-Private
Opened: 1991   *Architect:* Clyde Johnston

Greens fee:	$39.50 with cart daily; $49.50 weekends, holidays. Walking allowed.
Yardage:	Championship tees — 6,756
	Blue tees — 6,386
	Women's tees — 5,008
Course Rating:	Championship — 72.2
	Blues — 70.1
	Women's — 69.0

Comment: If you like long par 4s, you got 'em. Plus there are short par 4s that make you think. There are also no let-up par 3s, especially No. 16, 160-180 yards across the lake. Wicker baskets, not flags, adorn the flag sticks, which are a nice touch. You can't play this just once. It's too good. Word is it may become private at some point in 1993.

SOUTHLAND COUNTRY CLUB

Stone Mountain (404) 469-2717
Opened: 1988

18 holes, Par 72, Private
Architect: Willard Byrd

Yardage: Blue tees — 6,717
Women's tees — 5,028
Course Rating: Blues — 72.5
Women's — 69.1

SPRINGBROOK PUBLIC GOLF COURSE

Lawrenceville (404) 822-5400
Opened: 1968

18 holes, Par 71, Public
Architect: Perrin Walker

Greens fee: $25.73 with cart daily; $27.83 weekends, holidays. Walking allowed.

Yardage: Blue tees — 6,042
Women's tees — 4,738
Course Rating: Blues — 68.7
Women's — 67.1

Comment: This course has changed hands more often than a baton in a mile relay. It's now owned and operated by Gwinnett County. Short, moderately hilly, relatively easy, but you still have to hit the shots. An ego booster for the average player and perfect for those just beginning.

STANDARD CLUB

Duluth (404) 497-1920
Opened: 1987

18 holes, Par 72, Private
Architect: Arthur Hills

Yardage: Championship tees — 6,950
Blue tees — 6,372
Women's tees — 4,700
Course Rating: Championship — 73.5
Blues — 70.4
Women's — 67.2

STONE MOUNTAIN GOLF CLUB

Stone Mountain (404) 498-5715   36 holes, Par 72, Public

Green Fees: $36 with cart. Walking allowed at certain times.

WOODMONT/LAKEMONT
Opened: 1969   *Architects:* Robert Trent Jones/John LaFoy
Yardage: Blue tees — 6,595
          Women's tees — 5,231
Course Rating: Blues — 71.6
          Women's — 69.4

STONEMONT
Opened: 1992   *Architects:* Jones/LaFoy

Yardage: Blue tees — 6,683
          Women's — 5,020
Course Rating: Blues — 72.6
          Women's — 69.1

The mountain itself is the backdrop from this tee shot at Stone Mountain.

Comment: The original 18 designed by Robert Trent Jones is as good as it gets, and John LaFoy did a nice job with his adjoining nine. But the Lake nine isn't much, which isn't LaFoy's fault. He didn't have much land to work with; too many blind shots that lead to a bit of frustration, but not as much as having to pay to get into the park, then get hit with a $36 green fee.

SUGAR CREEK GOLF COURSE

Atlanta (404) 241-7671   18 holes, Par 72, Public
Opened: 1977   *Architect:* Evan Marbut

Greens fee:	$26 with cart daily; $29 weekends, holidays. Walking allowed.
Yardage:	Blue tees — 6,571 Women's tees — 5,679
Course Rating:	Blues — 71.6 Women's — 73.6

Comment: Owned and operated by DeKalb County, the course plays on both sides of I-285 — 11 on the east and seven on the west. It's a rather tough driving course, challenging with good Bermuda greens. Much of the course lies in the flood plain and therefore is almost unplayable after heavy rains.

SUGAR HILL GOLF CLUB

Sugar Hill (404) 271-0519   18 holes, Par 72, Public
Opened: 1992   *Architect:* Willard Byrd

Greens fee:	$28 with cart daily; $36 weekends, holidays. Walking allowed weekdays.
Yardage:	Blue tees — 6,423 Women's tees — 4,207
Course Rating:	Blues — 70.9 Women's — 65.3

Comment: Gwinnett County's second daily fee course is better than Springbrook. It plays longer than the 6,400 yards on the card. Accuracy is the key here, and if you can get through 14, 15 and 16 with pars, good job. The tee shot on each hole is over water to an elevated fairway and the second shots must be laser-like.

SUMMIT CHASE COUNTRY CLUB

Snellville (404) 979-9000   18 holes, Par 72, Private
Opened: 1973   *Architect:* Ward Northrup

Yardage:	Blue tees — 6,651
	Women's tees — 5,106
Course Rating:	Blues — 71.6
	Women's — 70.4

WEST PINES GOLF CLUB

Douglasville (404) 920-0850   18 holes, Par 71, Semi-Private
Opened: 1975   *Architect:* Unknown

Greens fee:	$20 with cart daily; $25 weekends, holidays. Walking allowed.
Yardage:	Blue tees — 6,500
	Women's tees — 4,835
Course Rating:	Blues — 70.9
	Women's — 67.3

WHITEWATER CREEK COUNTRY CLUB

Fayetteville (404) 461-6545   18 holes, Par 72, Semi-Private
Opened: 1986   *Architect:* Arnold Palmer

Greens fee: $32 with cart daily; $38 weekends, holidays.
                    No walking.

Yardage: Championship tees — 6,739
                    Blue tees — 6,284
                    Women's tees — 4,909
Course Rating: Championship — 72.3
                    Blues — 69.9
                    Women's — 68.8

Comment: You'll be hard pressed to find a more challenging course in the state, from the opening par 4 that demands a long tee shot to the closing 18th that invites you to go for it in two. The par 3s are especially difficult, with water coming into play on three of them. It takes an A-game to score well here.

WILLOW SPRINGS COUNTRY CLUB

Roswell (404) 475-7820   18 holes, Par 71, Private
Opened: 1974   *Architects:* Randy Nichols/Sam Smith

Yardage: Blue tees — 6,486
                    Women's tees — 5,031
Course Rating: Blues — 72.0
                    Women's — 69.5

East Georgia

ATHENS COUNTRY CLUB

Back in the early 1920s, Athens bragged about an 18-hole golf course called Cloverhurst Country Club. It had sand greens and tees and the par was only 63, but it was one of the sportiest layouts ever built in Georgia.

Well, Cloverhurst is no more, but Athens isn't without a sporty layout. Athens Country Club fits that description and more.

Donald Ross designed it, saying that the layout of the land was one of the most beautiful and well-suited for championship design of any course he had ever planned.

There were 103 bunkers on the original layout and par was 73 with a yardage of 6,554. The present yardage from the tips is 6,697 and par is 72. Mules and dragpans were used to build the course and lake.

This is a Donald Ross original and not many of them are left. Somebody is always trying to tinker with a Ross course, but Athens CC needs no tinkerers. Upon inaugurating the course on opening day, Bobby Jones described it as "a thing of beauty and a true test of golf."

No less an expert than Arnold Palmer still calls it one of his favorite courses. Palmer played it often during his college days at Wake Forest while competing in the Southern Intercollegiate Golf Tournament, which was organized in 1935 by the late Coach Herman Stegman and is still going strong today.

It's little wonder that the Georgia State Golf Association

has chosen Athens CC as the site of five State Amateurs, three since the Amateur went to medal play. Arnold Blum and Hugh Royer Jr. won it at match play; Bunky Henry, Lynn Lott and Paul Claxton won at medal play. Nobody has shot lower than 7-under for 72 holes.

The club added nine holes in 1985. Those nine are played with Ross's original 18, the South and East.

ATHENS COUNTRY CLUB

Athens (706) 354-7111   27 holes, Par 72, Private

EAST/SOUTH COURSE
Opened: 1926   *Architect:* Donald Ross

Yardage:	Championship tees — 6,697
	Blue tees — 6,436
	Women's tees — 5,495
Course Rating:	Championship — 72.9
	Blues — 71.7
	Women's — 72.2

NORTH NINE
Opened: 1985   *Architects:* George Cobb/John LaFoy

Yardage:	Championship tees — 3,253
	Blue tees — 3,032
	Women's tees — 2,432
Course Rating:	Championship — 36.3
	Blues — 35.3
	Women's — 34.7

AUGUSTA COUNTRY CLUB

Before there was Augusta National, wooden tees or grass greens, there was Augusta Country Club.

Augusta Country Club was founded in 1899. The course

design and construction was done by Dave Ogilvie, a Scotsman, and Dr. Fred Harrison, one of the club's founders.

The things we now take for granted were not to be found during those early years.

You think spike marks on greens are a nuisance. Try putting on sand, as the field of 200 did in the 1921 State Amateur, the biggest sporting event in Augusta history. It couldn't have been too bad. Montgomery Harrison, the eventual champion, was medalist with 78 on a course that measured almost 6,700 yards.

It wasn't until 1927 that the club hired Donald Ross to construct grass greens, but they couldn't have been much better than the sand ones. When the Amateur returned to Augusta in 1937, the medalist Dick Mulherin shot 73, only five shots better than on sand, and the champion, his brother Frank, qualified with 75.

Golf tees were years away. The tee boxes were constructed of hard clay and players built their tees from buckets of sand and water.

Augusta Country Club's greatest contribution to golf came in 1932. Needing money to help ends meet during the Depression, club members voted to sell an acre of its land for $200 to Augusta National, which was under construction. It wasn't just any old acre, however. Augusta National needed it to build the 12th hole and part of the 13th fairway. What a deal!

Two other bits of trivia involving Jones and Augusta Country Club:

In the year of his Grand Slam, 1930, Jones won the Southeastern Open at Augusta CC by 13 shots over Horton Smith.

In 1932, Jones made a hole-in-one on the 145-yard 14th. It was the last ace of his career, in which he made only two.

AUGUSTA COUNTRY CLUB

Augusta (706) 736-5322   18 holes, Par 72, Private
Opened: 1899   *Architect:* David Ogilvie/Donald Ross

Yardage:	Championship tees — 6,737
	Blue tees — 6,472
	Women's tees — 5,471
Course Rating:	Championship — 72.4
	Blues — 71.4
	Women's — 72.1

AUGUSTA NATIONAL

General consensus has it that Augusta National was built so one day there could be a Masters. Not so. The sole purpose was to have a course and organize a club primarily for men which would refrain from any kind of social activities not associated with golf.

Augusta National was Bobby Jones' baby. He wanted a course built to his own liking, one that utilized the natural advantages of the site chosen rather than resorting to artificiality. Plus he wanted it built in the South, not too far from Atlanta.

The result is one of the world's best courses and, of course, home of the Masters, the first of the four major championships, which is played each April.

It's hard to believe, but the Masters struggled in its early years. Tickets, which now are difficult to come by, were given away in those days, and members often put up the money for the purse. Jones was the drawing card. Though he quit playing competitively following his Grand Slam in 1930, Jones did participate in the nine pre-World War II Masters, but his finish was 13th in the first one, 1934.

Little known facts about Augusta National:

In the beginning, there were plans to sell a dozen estate

The most famous clubhouse in America — Augusta.

lots well back from the fairways. Only one lot was sold before Jones and club chairman Cliff Roberts had a change of heart.

Augusta was chosen for two reasons. It was the best place in Georgia for winter golf, and Jones wanted a very private place to play the game he loved.

There are only 29 bunkers. Jones liked mounds. Less maintenance and they often can be as penalizing.

Indian burial grounds were found on the site of the 12th green.

During the early 1930s, there was talk of holding a U.S. Open at Augusta National. Jones and Roberts said no thanks. They didn't want to set a precedent.

Jones did not like the name Masters and the tournament began as the Augusta National Invitational Tournament. It did not officially become the Masters until 1938.

The course was closed in 1943, '44 and '45 due to World War II. To help raise money, the club allowed cattle to graze and turkeys were raised. In late 1944, German soldiers, prisoners of war being held at Camp Gordon, were hired to rehabilitate the golf course.

The golf shot heard round the world came in 1935 when Gene Sarazan holed a 5-wood for eagle three, enabling him to tie Craig Wood. Sarazan won the title in an 18-hole playoff the next day.

AUGUSTA NATIONAL GOLF CLUB

Augusta (706) 733-9909   18 holes, Par 72, Private
Opened: 1932   *Architect:* Alister McKenzie

Yardage: Championship — 6,980
Course Rating: Not rated

BELLE MEADE COUNTRY CLUB

Thomson (706) 595-4511   18 holes, Par 72, Public
Opened: 1970   *Architect:* John LaFoy

Greens Fee: $20 with cart daily; $27 weekends, holidays. Walking allowed.

Yardage: Blue tee — 6,300
     Women's tees — 5,400
Course Rating: Blues — 69.9
     Women's — 65.6

CEDAR LAKE GOLF CLUB

Loganville (404) 466-4043   18 holes, Par 73, Public
Opened: 1986   *Architect:* Unknown

Greens Fee: $21 with cart daily; $27 weekends, holidays. Walking allowed.

Yardage:	Championship tees — 6,656
	Blue tees — 6,450
	Women's tees — 4,930
Course Rating:	Championship — 70.3
	Blues — 70.3
	Women's — 67.9

ELBERTON COUNTRY CLUB

Elberton (706) 283-5921   18 holes, Par 72, Private
Opened: 1946   *Architect:* Members

Yardage:	Blue tees — 6,320
	Women's tees — 5,360
Course Rating:	Blues — 68.7
	Women's — 68.8

FOREST HILLS GOLF CLUB

Augusta (706) 733-0001   18 holes, Par 72, Public
Opened: 1926   *Architect:* Donald Ross

Greens Fee:	$25 with cart daily; $32 weekends, holidays. Walking allowed.
Yardage:	Blue tees — 6,870
	Women's tees — 5,300
Course Rating:	Blues — 72.3
	Women's — 75.6

FOUR SEASONS GOLF CLUB

Wrens (706) 547-2816   9 holes, Par 36, Semi-Private
Opened: 1969   *Architect:* Swift-Gregg Assoc.

Greens Fee:	$13.50 with cart daily; $16.50 weekends, holidays. Walking allowed.
Yardage:	Blue tees — 3,099
	Women's tees — 2,516
Course Rating:	Not rated

GORDON LAKES GOLF COURSE

Ft. Gordon (706) 791-2433   18 holes, Par 72, Military (Private)
Opened: 1975   *Architect:* Robert Trent Jones

Yardage:	Blue tees — 7,077
	Women's tees (Par 73) — 5,881
Course Rating:	Blues — 74.0
	Women's — 73.7

GOSHEN PLANTATION CLUB

Augusta (706) 793-1168   18 holes, Par 72, Semi-Private
Opened: 1970   *Architect:* Ellis Maples

Greens Fee:	$20 with cart daily; $25 weekends, holidays. No walking.
Yardage:	Blue tees — 6,902
	Women's tees — 5,688
Course Rating:	Blues — 72.6
	Women's — 70.9

GREAT WATERS

Greensboro (706) 485-0235   18 Holes, Par 72, Semi-Private
Opened: 1992   *Architect:* Jack Nicklaus

Greens Fee:	$76 with cart Monday-Thursday; $86 Friday-Sunday. No walking.
Yardage:	Championship tees — 7,048
	Blue tees — 6,545
	Women's tees — 5,057
Course Rating:	Championship — 74.7
	Blues — 72.4
	Women's — 68.0

Comment: Destined to become one of the top 10 courses in the state and is the best new course in Georgia. Nine holes flank the shores of Lake Oconee. Unlike some of Nicklaus's courses, forced carries are rare and these greens have none of the sharp edges of his others. This is the most golfer-friendly resort course Nicklaus has designed. But play it while you can. It will probably become completely private in the future.

Great Waters 14th on Lake Oconee

GREENE COUNTY COUNTRY CLUB

Union Point (706) 486-4513   9 holes, Par 36, Private
Opened: 1966   *Architect:* Unknown

Yardage: Blue tees — 3,169
                            Women's tees — 2,500
Course Rating: Blues — 70.1
                            Women's — 68.4

GREEN HILLS COUNTRY CLUB

Athens (706) 548-6032   18 holes, Par 72, Semi-Private
Opened: 1959   *Architect:* Unknown

Greens Fee: $21.08 with cart daily; $25.08 weekends,
                     holidays. Walking allowed.

Yardage: Blue tees — 6,341
                     Women's tees — 5,201
Course Rating: Blues — 69.6
                     Women's — 68.2

HARBOR CLUB

Greensboro (706) 453-960   18 holes, Par 72, Private
Opened: 1991   *Architects:* Tom Weiskopf/Jay Morish

Yardage: Championship tees — 6,951
                     Blue tees — 6,458
                     Women's tees — 5,199
Course Rating: Championship — 73.7
                     Blues — 71.3
                     Women's — 70.2

HARD LABOR CREEK GOLF COURSE

Rutledge (706) 557-3006   18 holes, Par 72, Public
Opened: 1966   *Architect:* O.C. Jones

Greens Fee: $22.42 with cart. Walking allowed.

Yardage: Blue tees — 6,437
                     Women's tees — 4,854
Course Rating: Blues — 70.5
                     Women's — 67.3

Comment: Right away the name — Hard Labor — might scare
you away, but don't be intimidated. While it's tough, it's fair.

Overall, the course is a pretty good test. Tree-lined, small greens, well-bunkered and the rough isn't so rough anymore.

JENNINGS MILL COUNTRY CLUB

Athens (706) 548-1852   18 holes, Par 72, Private
Opened: 1987   *Architect:* Bob Cupp

Yardage: Championship tees — 6,924
                  Blue tees — 6,318
                  Women's tees — 5,232
Course Rating: Championship — 72.8
                  Blues — 70.4
                  Women's — 70.7

JONES CREEK GOLF CLUB

Augusta (706) 860-4228   18 holes, Par 72, Public
Opened: 1985   *Architect:* Rees Jones

Green Fees: $30 with cart daily; $40 weekends, holidays.
                  Walking allowed.

Yardage: Championship tees — 7,008
                  Blue tees — 6,557
                  Women's tees — 5,430
Course Rating: Championship — 73.8
                  Blues — 71.9
                  Women's — 72.4

Comment: If you like your golf courses to have one challenging hole after another, you'll love this Rees Jones layout. There are no let-ups, nor is there anything unfair about it. Just tee it up, grind away and beware of the creek. It's everywhere.

LANE CREEK GOLF CLUB

Bishop (706) 769-6699   18 holes, Par 72, Public
Opened: 1992   *Architect:* Mike Young

Greens fee:	$25 with cart daily; $30 weekends, holidays. Walking allowed.
Yardage:	Championship tees — 6,754 Blue tees — 6,349 Women's tees — 5,057
Course Rating:	Championship — 71.3 Blues — 69.3 Women's — 68.2

Comment: Mike Young, the architect, gives you a great variety of holes here. It's tough in spots, especially the 425-yard 13th, and though No. 4 is only 310 yards, it takes a delicate second shot over a pond to get to the green, where a bunker awaits those who are long.

MONROE GOLF & COUNTRY CLUB

Monroe (706) 267-8424   18 holes, Par 72, Semi-Private
Opened: 1957   *Architect:* Sam Crowe

Greens fee:	$29 with cart daily; $36 weekends, holidays. Walking allowed.
Yardage:	Blue tees — 6,300 Women's tees — 4,964
Course Rating:	Blues — 70.5 Women's — 68.9

PINE HILLS COUNTRY CLUB

Decatur (404) 981-1400   27 holes, Par 72, Private
Opened: 1972   *Architect:* Joe Lee

SUMMER/AUTUMN
Yardage: Blue tees — 6,658
                       Women's tees — 5,410
Course Rating: Blues — 71.7
                       Women's — 74.9

SPRING/SUMMER
Yardage: Blue tees — 6,684
                       Women's tees — 5,538
Course Rating: Blues — 71.7
                       Women's — 71.0

AUTUMN/SPRING
Yardage: Blue tees — 6,566
                       Women's tees — 5,394
Course Rating: Blues — 71.1
                       Women's — 70.6

POINTE SOUTH GOLF CLUB

Hephzibah (706) 592-2222   18 holes, Par 72, Semi-Private
Opened: 1991   *Architects:* Joe Clement/Ken Rivers

Greens fee: $23 with cart daily; $27 weekends, holidays.
                       Walking allowed weekdays.

Yardage: Blue tees — 6,324
                       Women's tees — 5,029
Course Rating: Blues — 69.1
                       Women's — 68.8

PORT ARMOR CLUB

Greensboro (706) 453-4564   18 holes, Par 72, Semi-Private
Opened: 1986   *Architect:* Bob Cupp

Greens Fee:	$75 with cart. Walking allowed after 3 p.m.
Yardage:	Championship tees — 6,926
	Blue tees — 6,285
	Women's tees — 5,177
Course Rating:	Championship — 73.6
	Blues — 70.6
	Women's — 70.8

Comment: One of the most demanding courses in Georgia, Port Armor will test not only your shot-making ability, but concentration, intestinal fortitude and disposition. Designer Bob Cupp makes you thread the needle on several short par 4s, but allows you to swing from the heels on the par 5s. The 378-yard par 4 fifth runs along the shore of Lake Oconee and is proof that holes don't have to be long to be great. If you don't like Port Armor, you don't like golf.

REYNOLDS PLANTATION

Greensboro (706) 467-3159   18 holes, Par 72, Semi-private
Opened: 1988   *Architects:* Bob Cupp/Fuzzy Zoeller/Hubert Green

Green Fees:	Tuesday-Thursday, $56 with cart; Friday-Sunday, $61. No walking.
Yardage:	Blue tees — 6,656
	Women's tees — 5,162
Course Rating:	Blues — 71.2
	Women's — 69.1

Comment: The best description of Reynolds Plantation is golfer-friendly. Bob Cupp did most of the design with consultation from Fuzzy Zoeller and Hubert Green. Their effort provided the average golfer with a course he can play with a minimum of frustration. The lone negative is No. 10, a par 4 that only the long hitters *can appreciate.*

THOMSON COUNTRY CLUB

Thomson (706) 595-2727   9 holes, Par 72, Semi-Private
Opened: 1962   *Architect:* Unknown

Greens fee:	$13.50 with cart daily; $18.50 weekends, holidays. Walking allowed.
Yardage:	Blue tees — 6,218 Women's tees — 5,432
Course Rating:	Blues — 69.5 Women's — 70.1

TURTLE COVE COUNTRY CLUB

Monticello (706) 468-8805   9 holes, Par 60, Private
Opened: 1972   *Architect:* Unknown

Yardage:	Blue tees — 4,030 Women's tees — 3,560
Course Rating:	Blues — 58.9 Women's — 59.7

UNCLE REMUS GOLF COURSE

Eatonton (706) 485-6850   9 holes, Par 36, Public
Opened: 1960   *Architect:* Unknown

Greens fee:	$14 with cart daily; $16 weekends, holidays. Walking allowed.
Yardage:	Blue tees — 3,390 Women's tees — 2,480
Course Rating:	Blues — 71.2 Women's — Not rated

UNIVERSITY OF GEORGIA GOLF COURSE

Athens (706) 369-5739	18 holes, Par 72, Public
Opened: 1968	*Architect:* Robert Trent Jones

Greens fee: $24.50 with cart daily; $26.50 weekends, holidays. Walking allowed.

Yardage: Championship tees — 6,890
Blue tees — 6,495
Women's tees — 6,083

Course Rating: Championship — 73.4
Blues — 71.5
Women's — 76.4

Comment: This isn't one of those pitch and putt courses you see in some college towns. This is a GOLF COURSE. Every hole is good, especially those that play along the lake, and No. 18 is an All-American closing par 4.

WASHINGTON-WILKES COUNTRY CLUB

Washington (706) 678-2046	9 holes, Par 72, Private
Opened: 1925	*Architect:* Donald Ross

Yardage: Blue tees — 6,496
Women's tees — 5,058

Course Rating: Blues — 70.2
Women's — 68.4

WAYNESBORO COUNTRY CLUB

Waynesboro (706) 554-2262	18 holes, Par 72, Private
Opened: 1926	*Architect:* George Cobb

Yardage: Blue tees — 6,834
Women's tees — 4,707

Course Rating: Blues — 68.0
Women's — 58.0

WEST LAKE COUNTRY CLUB

Augusta (706) 863-4642   18 holes, Par 72, Private
Opened: 1969   *Architect:* Eric Maples/John LaFoy

Yardage: Championship tees — 6,876
                Blue tees — 6,354
                Women's tees — 5,318
Course Rating: Championship — 73.3
                Blues — 70.7
                Women's — 65.8

WHISPERING PINES GOLF COURSE

Colbert (706) 788-2720   18 holes, Par 72, Public
Opened: First 9 - 1970;   *Architect:* David Green, Jack Rhodes
         Second 9 - 1980

Greens fee: $22 with cart daily; $24 weekends, holidays.
                Walking allowed.

Yardage: Championship tees — 6,387
                Blue tees — 5,856
                Women's tees — 4,701
Course Rating: Championship — 69.9
                Blues — 69.7
                Women's — 67.5

Loading up for a busy Saturday at Brookfield.

West Georgia

AMERICAN LEGION GOLF CLUB

LaGrange (706) 884-4379   9 holes, Par 36, Public
Opened: 1960   *Architect:* Max McKay

Greens fee:	$15.50 with cart daily; $19.50 weekends, holidays. Walking allowed.
Yardage:	Blue tees — 3,085
	Women's tees — None
Course Rating:	Blues — 69.1

CANONGATE-ON-WHITE OAK

Newnan (706) 251-6700   36 holes, Par 72, Private

THE OLD COURSE
Opened: 1986   *Architect:* Rocky Roquemore

Yardage:	Championship tees — 6,802
	Blue tees — 6,356
	Women's tees — 5,259
Course Rating:	Championship — 72.4
	Blues — 70.4
	Women's — 70.1

SEMINOLE
Opened: 1990   *Architect:* Rocky Roquemore

Yardage:	Championship tees — 6,561
	Blue tees — 6,231
	Women's tees — 5,053
Course Rating:	Championship — 71.5
	Blues — 70.2
	Women's — 68.7

THE FIELDS AT ROSEMONT HILLS

LaGrange (706) 845-7425   18 holes, Par 72, Public
Opened: 1991   *Architects:* Mike Young/Mitch Bourgeious

Greens fee:	$24 with cart daily; $27 weekends, holidays. Walking allowed weekdays and after 4 p.m. weekends, holidays.
Yardage:	Blue tees — 6,600 Women's tees — 4,922
Course Rating:	Blues — 71.4 Women's — 67.0

HIGHLAND COUNTRY CLUB

LaGrange (706) 882-3026   18 holes, Par 72, Private
Opened: 1922   *Architects:* Donald Ross/Joe Fingers

Yardage:	Blue tees — 6,563 Women's tees — 5,314
Course Rating:	Blues — 71.3 Women's — 70.7

MAPLE CREEK GOLF COURSE

Bremen (706) 537-4172   18 holes, Par 70, Public
Opened: 1992   *Architect:* Unknown

Greens Fee:	$19 with cart daily; $21 weekends, holidays. Walking allowed.
Yardage:	Blue tees — 5,303 Women's tees — 4,454
Course Rating:	Blues — 66.3 Women's — 64.9

NEWNAN COUNTRY CLUB

Newnan (706) 253-3675
18 holes, Par 72, Private
Opened: 1919
Architect: Unknown

Yardage: Blue tees — 6,966
                    Women's tees — 5,337
Course Rating: Blues — 73.7
                    Women's — 69.9

ORCHARD HILLS GOLF CLUB

Newnan (706) 251-5683
18 holes, Par 72, Public
Opened: 1990
Architect: Don Cottle Jr.

Greens fee: $30 with cart daily; $35 weekends, holidays. Walking allowed.

Yardage: Championship tees — 6,909
                    Blue tees — 6,530
                    Women's tees — 5,304
Course Rating: Championship — 72.9
                    Blues — 71.2
                    Women's — 69.5

Comment: There's nothing not to like about this Scottish-looking layout. It gives the good golfer all he can handle from the back tees and is very playable from the blues. It's a wide course, water comes into play on only five holes, and the 28 bunkers are hardly menacing. Tremendous greens. Great place for a company outing.

THE PLANTATION COUNTRY CLUB

Villa Rica (706) 830-8616
18 holes, Par 72, Private
Opened: 1973
Architect: Willard Byrd

Yardage: Blue tees — 6,612
                    Women's tees — 5,358
Course Rating: Blues — 72.5
                    Women's — 72.2

Links-like Orchard Hills is testy and forgiving.

SUNSET HILLS COUNTRY CLUB

Carrollton (706) 832-2441   18 holes, Par 71, Private
Opened: 1942   *Architect:* Robert Trent Jones

Yardage: Blue tees — 6,300
     Women's tees — 5,070
Course Rating: Blues — 70.0
     Women's — 68.9

TALLAPOOSA CITY MOUNTAIN GOLF COURSE

Tallapoosa (706) 574-3122   9 holes, Par 72, Public
Opened: 1967   *Architect:* Unknown

Greens fee: $14 with cart daily; $20 weekends, holidays.
     Walking allowed.

Yardage: Blue tees — 6,308
     Women's tees — 5,214
Course Rating: Blues — 69.0
     Women's — 65.7

Loaded up, ready to go.

Practice, practice, practice!

Middle Georgia

BARRINGTON HALL GOLF CLUB

Macon (912) 757-8358   18 holes, Par 72, Semi-Private
Opened: 1992   *Architect:* Tom Clark

Greens fee:	$22 with cart daily; $29 weekends, holidays. Walking allowed.
Yardage:	Championship tees — 7,062 Blue tees — 6,645 Women's tees — 5,012
Course Rating:	Championship — 72.3 Blues — 71.0 Women's — 69.1

Comment: For a new course, it's getting rave reviews. It's no chip and putt place. Water comes into play on almost half the holes; it's tight; and you can't see the greens from the tees on most of the back nine.

BEAVER LAKE GOLF & COUNTRY CLUB

Gay (706) 538-6994   18 holes, Par 72, Semi-Private
Opened: 1964   *Architect:* Unknown

Greens Fee:	$13 with cart daily; $20 weekends, holidays. Walking allowed.
Yardage:	Blue tees — 6,672 Women's tees — 5,241
Course Rating:	Blues — 72.4 Women's — 70.1

BOWDEN GOLF COURSE

Macon (912) 742-1610   18 holes, Par 72, Public
Opened: 1939   *Architect:* Dick Cotton

Greens Fee:	$24.75 with cart daily; $25.75 weekends, holidays. Walking allowed.
Yardage:	Blue tees — 6,620 Women's tees — 4,775
Course Rating:	Blues — 69.7 Women's — 66.4

BULL CREEK GOLF COURSE

Columbus (706) 561-1614   36 holes, Par 72, Public
Opened: 1972   *Architect:* Joe Lee

Greens Fee:	$21.63 with cart daily; $23.73 weekends, holidays. Walking allowed.

EAST COURSE

Yardage:	Championship tees — 6,705 Blue tees — 6,420 Women's tees — 5,430
Course Rating:	Championship — 72.7 Blues — 71.3 Women's — 69.5

WEST COURSE

Yardage:	Championship tees — 6,921 Blue tees — 6,480 Women's tees — 5,385
Course Rating:	Will be rated in 1993

Comment: These are some of the finest municipal courses in the state and the most affordable for the public golfer. There is a great balance of holes with no gimme birdies on any of them. These courses demand accuracy off the tee and precision shots to the Bermuda greens, where reading the grain is a challenge to even the most experienced eye.

CABIN CREEK GOLF CLUB

Griffin (706) 227-9794   18 holes, Par 72, Private
Opened: 1973   *Architect:* Unknown

Yardage: Championship tees — 6,800
               White tees — 6,543
               Women's tees — 5,206 (par 71)
Course Rating: Championship — 69.5
               White — 69.1
               Women's — 68.9

CALHOUN ELKS GOLF CLUB

Calhoun (706) 629-4091   18 holes, Par 71, Semi-Private
Opened: 1953   *Architect:* Redesigned by several

Greens Fee: $16 with cart daily; $20 weekends, holidays.
               Walking allowed.

Yardage: Blue tees — 6,100
               Women's tees — 4,600
Course Rating: Blues — 67.6
               Women's — 65.0

CALLAWAY GARDENS

Callaway Gardens has three 18-hole courses and a nine-hole executive layout that is perfect for those just starting the game or for working on your short game.

The Lakeview course isn't long, but don't be misled by its length. The lake comes into play often enough to make it interesting and equally challenging.

Garden View is only moderately difficult, but is the most scenic with its fairways trailing along the orchards and vineyards and gardens.

The heart and soul of Callaway Gardens is the Dick

Wilson-designed Mountain View course, home of the PGA Tour's Buick Southern Open. The pros ranked it the second best conditioned resort course — TPC Sawgrass was No. 1 — they played in 1992. And it's not one of those courses where the pros have to shoot 20-under to win.

Single digit handicappers will have their hands full from the back tees, and the high handicapper is advised to play from the most forward tees.

CALLAWAY GARDENS

Pine Mountain (706) 663-2281   63 holes, Par varies, Resort

Greens Fee: Nov.-Mar. — Mountain View $65 with cart.
                    Gardens View/Lake View $50 with cart.
                    April-Oct. — Mountain View $75 with cart.
                    Gardens View/Lake View $60 with cart.
                    Walking allowed during summer on
                    Gardens View and Lake View after 4 p.m.

MOUNTAIN VIEW
Opened: 1964   *Architect:* Dick Wilson/Joe Lee

Yardage: Championship tees — 7,057
                Blue tees — 6,630
                Women's tees — 5,848
Course Rating: Championship — 74.1
                Blues — 72.3
                Women's — 73.2

LAKE VIEW
Opened: First 9 in 1951,   *Architects:* Dick Wilson/J.B. McGovern
          second in '62

Yardage: Blue tees — 6,006
                Women's tees — 5,452
Course Rating: Blues — 69.4
                Women's — 70.3

GARDENS VIEW
Opened: 1969   *Architect:* Joe Lee

Yardage:	Championship tees — 6,392
	Blue tees — 6,108
	Women's tees — 5,848
Course Rating:	Championship — 70.7
	Blues — 69.2
	Women's — 72.7

SKY VIEW (9-hole Executive)
Opened: 1967   *Architects:* Dick Wilson/Joe Lee

Yardage:	Championship tees — 2,096
	Blue tees — 1,961
	Women's tees — 1,220
Course Rating:	Not rated

Callaway Gardens is home to the Buick Southern Open.

CEDAR CREEK GOLF & COUNTRY CLUB

Buena Vista (912) 649-3381   9 holes, Par 72, Semi-Private
Opened: 1972   *Architect:* Unknown

Greens Fee:	$15 with cart daily; $17 weekends, holidays. Walking allowed weekdays.
Yardage:	Blue tees — 6,510
	Women's tees — 4,652
Course Rating:	Blues — 71.0
	Women's — 70.0

CEDARS GOLF CLUB

Zebulon (706) 567-8808   18 holes, Par 72, Semi-Private
Opened: 1965   *Architect:* Unknown

Greens Fee:	$19 with cart daily; $24 weekends, holidays. Walking allowed daily and after 1 p.m. weekends, holidays.
Yardage:	Blue tees — 6,513
	Women's tees — 5,292
Course Rating:	Blues — 70.9
	Women's — 70.1

COUNTRY CLUB OF COLUMBUS

(706) 322-6869   18 holes, Par 71, Private
Opened: 1909   *Architect:* Donald Ross

Yardage:	Blue tees — 6,391
	Women's tees — 4,974
Course Rating:	Blues — 71.1
	Women's — 71.0

DEER TRAIL COUNTRY CLUB

Barnesville (706) 358-0349   18 holes, Par 72, Private
Opened: 1981   *Architect:* Unknown

Yardage: Blue tees — 6,750
                        Ladies tees — 5,320
Course Rating: Blues — 71.6
                        Women's — Not rated

DUBLIN COUNTRY CLUB

Dublin (912) 272-1549   18 holes, Par 72, Private
Opened: 1948   *Architect:* Tom Birdsong redesign

Yardage: Championship tees — 6,628
                        Blue tees — 6,343
                        Women's tees — 5,335
Course Rating: Championship — 71.8
                        Blues — 70.8
                        Women's — 71.6

FOLLOW ME GOLF COURSE

Ft. Benning (706) 687-1940   36 holes, Par 72, Private

PINESIDE
Opened: 1925   *Architect:* Lester Lawrence

Yardage: Blue tees — 6,606
                        Women's tees — 5,547
Course Rating: Blues — 71.6
                        Women's — 70.6

FORSYTH COUNTRY CLUB

Forsyth (912) 994-5328   18 holes, Par 72, Public
Opened: 1935   *Architect:* Unknown

Greens fee: $15.75 with cart daily; $17.85 weekends,
                  holidays. Walking allowed after 3 p.m.

Yardage: Blue tees — 6,300
                  Women's tees — 5,018
Course Rating: Blues — 68.1
                  Women's — 65.4

GOLF CLUB OF MACON

Macon (912) 474-8080   18 holes, Par 70, Private
Opened: 1962   *Architect:* Unknown

Yardage: Blue tees — 6,003
                  Women's tees — 5,014
Course Rating: Blues — 67.8
                  Women's — 67.1

GREEN ISLAND COUNTRY CLUB

Columbus (706) 324-3706   18 holes, Par 70, Private
Opened: 1962   *Architect:* George Cobb

Yardage: Championship tees — 6,687
                  Blue tees — 6,129
                  Women's — 5,251
Course Rating: Championship — 72.8
                  Blues — 70.7
                  Women's — 72.3

GREEN VALLEY GOLF CLUB

McDonough (404) 957-2800   18 holes, Par 72, Public
Opened: 1977   *Architect:* Unknown

Greens Fee:	$21 with cart daily; $25 weekends, holidays. Walking allowed weekdays and after 1 p.m. weekends, holidays.
Yardage:	Blue tees — 6,200 Women's tees — 5,500
Course Rating:	Blues — 69.4 Women's — 71.5

GRIFFIN COUNTRY CLUB

Griffin (706) 228-4744   18 holes, Par 72, Private
Opened: 1968   *Architect:* Willard Byrd

Yardage:	Blue tees — 6,821 Women's tees — 5,520
Course Rating:	Blues — 73.3 Women's — 71.6

GRIFFIN GOLF COURSE

Griffin (706) 229-6615   18 holes, Par 72, Public
Opened: 1933   *Architect:* Unknown

Greens Fee:	$21 with cart daily; $24.15 weekends, holidays. Walking allowed.
Yardage:	Blue tees — 6,790 Women's tees — 5,539
Course Rating:	Blues — 71.4 Women's — 69.9

HICKORY HILL GOLF COURSE

Jackson (706) 775-2433   18 holes, Par 71, Private
Opened: 1966   *Architect:* Allen Byars

Yardage:	Blue tees — 6,027
	Women's tees — 5,495
Course Rating:	Not rated

HOLIDAY HILLS GOLF CLUB

Gordon (912) 628-5150   18 holes, Par 70, Private
Opened: 1967   *Architect:* P. McNeil

Yardage:	Blue tees — 5,344
	Women's tees — 4,726
Course Rating:	Blues — 64.9
	Women's — 66.2

HOUSTON LAKE COUNTRY CLUB

Perry (912) 987-3243   18 holes, Par 72, Semi-Private
Opened: 1965   *Architects:* O.C. Jones/Brent Whitley

Greens fee:	$26 with cart daily; $36 weekends, holidays. No walking.
Yardage:	Championship tees — 6,600
	Blue tees — 6,400
	Women's tees — 5,100
Course Rating:	Championship — 71.7
	Blues — 70.7
	Women's — 70.0

Comment: One of middle Georgia's best. You don't have to be long, but you better be accurate. The par 3s are strong and No. 18, a 420-yard par 4, is included on the list of Georgia's Best 18. The other 17 at Houston Lake aren't bad either.

HUNTER POPE COUNTRY CLUB

Monticello (706) 468-6222   18 holes, Par 72, Semi-Private
Opened: 1967   *Architect:* Mike Young

Greens fee:	$16 with cart daily; $20 weekends, holidays. Walking allowed weekdays.
Yardage:	Blue tees — 6,050
	Women's tees — 4,440
Course Rating:	Blues — 67.4
	Women's — 65.9

IDLE HOUR

Idle Hour Golf Club traces its beginning to around 1890, when tennis was the most popular sport of Macon's gentry. It wasn't until the early 1900s that a nine-hole course was roughed out.

The property where the club now stands was a stock farm owned by R.H. Plant, whose interest was in raising trotters, not hitting a golf ball. He had one of the finest one mile dirt tracks south of Louisville, Kentucky. Plant named his stock farm Idle Hour because he spent so many idle hours there.

The first nine holes were opened in 1914, but the ground had been partially stripped of turf for improvement of the race track. The fairways were literally covered with rocks, and the early golfers would come out on weekends and play what they called "Rock Foursomes." After hitting a shot, they would pick up rocks all the way to their next shot. Mounds of rock were raked up into the rough and there was no penalty for lifting out of the rock piles.

Gradually a second nine was carved out of a solid forest of trees, and again it was the members who did the work. In those days, the course continuously played as ground under repair, but by the early 1920s was presentable enough for competition.

The remains of the horse track are still visible. Traces can be seen along the right side of No. 6, in the fairway of No. 11 near the green and through the woods along the No. 9 rough.

Idle Hour has been host to five State Amateur Championships, the first in 1923, when East Lake's Watts Gunn defeated Charles Black 1-up.

Idle Hour's gift to state golf is Arnold Bloom, who won five state titles between 1946 and 1956. But he never won on his home course, finishing second to Jennings Gordon in 1940 and E. Harvie Ward Jr. in 1953. Bloom had won three straight until Ward stopped his streak.

Bloom still holds the record for consecutive victories and held the mark for most titles — five — until Allen Doyle eclipsed it with his sixth in 1988. Ironically, Doyle won his first championship at Idle Hour in 1978, the last year the tournament was held there.

In one of the most exciting Amateurs of 1968, Toby Browne, now head professional at the Savannah Golf Club, defeated former PGA Tour player Steve Melnyk with a birdie on the first hole of sudden death. A year later, Melynk won the U.S. Amateur at Oakmont Country Club in Pittsburgh.

IDLE HOUR GOLF AND COUNTRY CLUB

Macon (912) 477-2092	18 holes, Par 71, Private
Opened: 1919	*Architect:* The members

Yardage:	Championship tees — 6,448
	Blue tees — 6,120
	Women's tees — 5,195
Course Rating:	Championship — 71.1
	Blues — 69.6
	Women's — 70.8

INTERNATIONAL CITY COURSE

Warner Robins (912) 922-3892
Opened: 1957

18 holes, Par 70, Public
Architect: Unknown

Greens fee: $17.85 with cart daily; $21 weekends, holidays. Walking allowed.

Yardage: Blue tees — 5,684
Women's tees — 4,082

Course Rating: Blues — 65.3
Women's — 60.9

LANDINGS GOLF CLUB

Warner Robins (912) 923-5222
Opened: 1987

27 holes, Semi-private
Architect: Edmond Ault

Green fees: $27.90 with cart daily; $33.15 weekends, holidays. Walking allowed.

Yardage: Championship tees — 6,998
Blue tees — 6,621
Women's tees — 5,698

Course Rating: Championship — 73.1
Blues — 71.6
Women's — 72.0

CREEK (nine holes)
Opened: 1990   *Architect:* Alan White

Yardage: Championship tees — 3,246
Blue tees — 3,121
Women's tees — 2,485

Course Rating: Not rated

LITTLE FISHING CREEK

Milledgeville (912) 452-9072   18 holes, Par 72, Public
Opened: 1981   *Architect:* Gary Player Corp.

Greens fee:	$15.75 with cart daily; $17.85 weekends, holidays. Walking allowed.
Yardage:	Blue tees — 6,718 Women's tees — 5,509
Course Rating:	Blues — 72.4 Women's — 73.6

MILLEDGEVILLE COUNTRY CLUB

Milledgeville (912) 452-3220   18 holes, Par 72, Private
Opened: 1960   *Architect:* George Cobb

Yardage:	Blue tees — 6,242 Women's tees — 4,860
Course Rating:	Blues — 70.0 Women's — 68.6

PEBBLEBROOK GOLF CLUB

Woodbury (706) 846-3809   9 holes, Par 72, Public
Opened: 1970   *Architect:* Arthur Davis

Greens fee:	$14.25 with cart daily; $18.25 weekends, holidays. Walking allowed.
Yardage:	Blue tees — 6,322 Women's tees — 5,308
Course Rating:	Blues — 68.7 Women's — 70.1

PERRY COUNTRY CLUB

Perry (912) 987-1033

18 holes, Par 71, Private

Opened: 1952

Architect: Sid Clark

Yardage:	Blue tees — 6,789
	Women's tees — 5,622
Course Rating:	Blues — 71.6
	Women's — 71.0

PINE NEEDLES COUNTRY CLUB

Ft. Valley (912) 825-3816

9 holes, Par 72, Private

Opened: 1942

Architect: Brissom Dang

Yardage:	Blue tees — 6,156
	Women's tees — 5,054
Course Rating:	Blues — 68.8
	Women's — 68.3

PINE OAKS GOLF COURSE

Warner Robins (912) 923-7334

18 holes, Par 71, Military

Opened: 1956

Architect: Military

Yardage:	Blue tees — 6,343
	Women's tees — 5,530
Course Rating:	Blues — 71.0
	Women's — 73.1

PINES GOLF CLUB

Williamson (706) 229-4107   18 holes, Par 72, Public
Opened: 1965   *Architect:* Unknown

Greens Fee: $19 with cart daily; $24 weekends, holidays.
                            Walking allowed daily and after 1 p.m.
                            weekends, holidays.

Yardage: Blue tees — 6,139
                            Women's tees — 5,038
Course Rating: Blues — 67.9
                            Women's — 67.7

RED OAK GOLF CLUB

Cusseta (404) 989-3312   18 holes, Par 71, Public
Opened: 1991   *Architect:* Lynn Page

Greens fee: $18 with cart daily; $21 weekends, holidays.
                            Walking allowed.

Yardage: Blue tees — 6,400
                            Women's tees — 4,765
Course Rating: Not rated

RIVER NORTH COUNTRY CLUB

Macon (912) 743-1495   18 holes, Par 72, Private
Opened: 1972   *Architect:* Gary Player

Yardage: Championship tees — 6,714
                            Blue tees — 6,293
                            Women's tees — 5,043
Course Rating: Championship — 72.4
                            Blues — 70.6
                            Women's — 69.5

RIVERSIDE GOLF & COUNTRY CLUB

Macon (912) 477-6764   18 holes, Par 72, Private
Opened: 1959   *Architect:* Unknown

Yardage: Blue tees — 6,773
                    Women's tees — 5,072
Course Rating: Blues — 72.0
                    Women's — 68.0

RIVERVIEW PARK GOLF COURSE

Dublin (912) 275-4064   18 holes, Par 72, Public
Opened: 1977   *Architect:* Unknown

Greens fee: $23 with cart daily; $24 weekends, holidays.
                    Walking allowed.

Yardage: Blue tees — 6,041
                    Women's tees — 5,020
Course Rating: Blues — 67.7
                    Women's — 67.3

ROOSEVELT MEMORIAL GOLF CLUB

Warm Springs (706) 655-5230   9 holes, Par 70, Public
Opened: 1926   *Architect:* Donald Ross

Greens fee: $22 with cart. Walking allowed weekdays.

Yardage: Blue tees — 6,198
                    Women's tees — 5,218
Course Rating: Blues — 72.0
                    Women's — 72.0

THOMASTON COUNTRY CLUB

Thomaston (706) 647-7358   9 holes, Par 72, Private
Opened: 1939   *Architect:* Unknown

Yardage: Blue tees — 6,160
                    Women's tees — 5,286
Course Rating: Blues — 69.5
                    Women's — 70.0

UCHEE TRAIL COUNTRY CLUB

Cochran (912) 934-7891   9 holes, Par 72, Private
Opened: 1969   *Architect:* Unknown

Yardage: Blue tees — 7,018
                    Women's tees — 5,468
Course Rating: Blues — 74.4
                    Women's — 72.2

WATERFORD GOLF CLUB

Bonaire (912) 328-7533   18 holes, Par 72, Semi-Private
Opened: 1991   *Architect:* Don Cottle Jr.

Greens fee: $21 with cart daily; $24.15 weekends,
                    holidays. Walking allowed.

Yardage: Championship tees — 6,400
                    Blue tees — 6,100
                    Women's tees — 5,600
Course Rating: Championship — 68.9
                    Blues — 67.6
                    Women's — 69.5

Comment: Short, relatively forgiving and open. Some tee shots
are blind, and water can make you a little nervous on the par 5
15th and par 3 17th. It's a nice little golf course that the
beginners will enjoy.

THE WOODS GOLF COURSE

Cochran (912) 934-0731   18 holes, Par 72, Public
Opened: 1989   *Architects:* Charlton Norris,
Charles Thompson Jr.,
Gary Norris, Tom Norris

Greens fee: $13.25 with cart. Walking allowed weekdays only.

Yardage: Blue tees — 6,061
Women's tees — 4,826

Course Rating: Not yet Rated

Beware the swamp at Georgia Veterans Park.

South Georgia

AMERICAN LEGION CLUB

Albany (912) 432-6016   9 holes, Par 35, Public
Opened: 1920   *Architect:* Unknown

Greens Fee:	$14.40 with cart daily; $15.40 weekends, holidays. Walking allowed.
Yardage:	Blue tees — 2,819 Women's tees — 2,438
Course Rating:	Blues — 66.8 Women's — 67.8

AMERICUS COUNTRY CLUB

Americus (912) 924-2914   18 holes, Par 72, Private
Opened: 1946   *Architect:* Unknown

Yardage:	Blue tees — 6,200 Women's — 5,800
Course Rating:	Blues — 70.9 Women's — 68.4

APPLING COUNTRY CLUB

Baxley (912) 367-3582   9 holes, Par 72, Semi-Private
Opened: 1962   *Architect:* Unknown

Greens Fee:	$15 with cart daily; $17 weekends, holidays. Walking allowed.
Yardage:	Blue tees — 6,652 Women's tees — 5,006
Course Rating:	Blues — 72.9 Women's — 68.0

BACON PARK GOLF COURSE

Savannah (912) 354-2625   27 holes, Par 72, Public
Opened: 1926   *Architect:* Donald Ross

Greens Fee: $20.30 with cart daily; $22.40 weekends, holidays. Walking allowed Mon.-Thurs. and after 1:30 weekends, holidays.

LIVE OAK-TO-MAGNOLIA
Yardage: Blue tees — 6,679
                  Women's tees — 5,160
Course Rating: Blues — 70.7
                  Women's — 69.4

CYPRESS-TO-LIVE OAK
Yardage: Blue tees — 6,573
                  Women's — 4,943
Course Rating: Blues — 70.5
                  Women's — 68.3

CYPRESS-TO-MAGNOLIA
Yardage: Blue tees — 6,740
                  Women's tees — 5,309
Course Rating: Blues — 69.9
                  Women's — 66.9

Comment: If you want a good taste of what the famous course designer Donald Ross was all about, you'll find it on these courses. They're simple, but testing, especially the small greens with their inverted saucer shape. American Golf Corp. keeps them in excellent condition. They are one of Georgia's best buys in golf.

BAINBRIDGE COUNTRY CLUB

Bainbridge (912) 246-1986   18 holes, Par 72, Private
Opened: 1923   *Architect:* Les Hall

Yardage: Blue tees — 6,540
                  Women's — 5,489

Course Rating: Blues — 69.1
                   Women's — 70.5

BEAVER KREEK GOLF CLUB

Douglas (912) 384-8230   18 holes, Par 72, Semi-Private
Opened: 1988   *Architect:* Ray Jensen/Kirby Holton

Greens Fee: $24.15 with cart. Walking allowed at non-
                   peak times.

Yardage: Championship tees — 6,543
                   Blue tees — 6,220
                   Women's tees — 5,414
Course Rating: To be rated in 1993

BRAZELL'S CREEK GOLF COURSE

Reidsville (912) 557-6445   9 holes, Par 36, Public
Opened: 1991   *Architect:* David Nelson

Greens Fee: $20.42 with cart. Walking allowed.

Yardage: Blue tees — 6,115
                   Women's tees — 5,000
Course Rating: Blues — 69.0
                   Women's — 69.0

BRIAR CREEK COUNTRY CLUB

Sylvania (912) 863-4161   9 holes, Par 36, Private
Opened: 1921   *Architect:* Unknown

Yardage: Blue tees — 3,319
                   Women's — 2,809
Course Rating: Blues — 71.2
                   Women's — 70.6

BRICKYARD PLANTATION GOLF CLUB

Americus (912) 874-1234   27 holes, Par 72, Semi-Private
Opened: 1979   *Architect:* W.N. Clark

Greens Fee: $20 with cart daily. Walking allowed.

DITCHES
Yardage: Blue tees — 3,176
     Women's tees — 2,737
Course Rating: Not rated

WATERS
Yardage: Blue tees — 2,938
     Women's tees — 2,544
Course Rating: Not rated

MOUNDS
Yardage: Blue tees — 3,292
     Women's tees — 2,655
Course Rating: Not rated

BRUNSWICK COUNTRY CLUB

Brunswick (912) 264-0331   18 holes, Par 72, Private
Opened: 1934   *Architect:* Donald Ross

Yardage: Blue tees — 6,782
     Women's tees — 5,470
Course Rating: Blues — 71.1
     Women's — 71.0

CAIRO COUNTRY CLUB

Cairo (912) 377-4506   18 holes, Par 72, Private
Opened: 1960   *Architect:* Julian Rodenberry Jr.

Yardage: Blue tees — 6,764
     Women's tees — 5,661
Course Rating: Blues — 71.8
     Women's — 71.9

CHEROKEE ROSE COUNTRY CLUB

Hinesville (912) 876-5503   18 holes, Par 71, Public
Opened: 1971   *Architect:* Unknown

Greens Fee: $18.55 with cart daily; $23.85 weekends,
                     holidays. Walking allowed.

Yardage: Blue tees — 6,101
                     Women's tees — 4,711
Course Rating: Blues — 69.9
                     Women's — 67.3

CIRCLESTONE COUNTRY CLUB

Adel (912) 896-3893   9 holes, Par 36, Private
Opened: 1961   *Architect:* Unknown

Yardage: Blue tees — 3,201
                     Women's tees — 2,707
Course Rating: Blues — 69.8
                     Women's — 69.8

COUNTRY OAKS GOLF COURSE

Thomasville (912) 225-4333   18 holes, Par 72, Public
Opened: 1979   *Architect:* Ray Jenson

Greens Fee: $16.28 with cart daily; $18.38 weekends,
                     holidays. Walking allowed.

Yardage: Blue tees — 6,193
                     Women's tees — 5,196
Course Rating: Blues — 70.3
                     Women's — 70.2

DAWSON COUNTRY CLUB

Dawson (912) 995-2255   9 holes, Par 36, Private
Opened: 1950   *Architect:* Unknown

Yardage: Blue tees — 3,162
                    Women's tees — 2,499
Course Rating: Blues — 69.8
                    Women's — 68.4

DODGE COUNTY GOLF CLUB

Eastman (912) 374-3616   9 holes, Par 72, Private
Opened: 1954   *Architect:* Unknown

Yardage: Blue tees — 2,982
                    Women's tees — 2,651
Course Rating: Blues — 67.3
                    Women's — 69.0

DONALSONVILLE COUNTRY CLUB

Donalsonville (912) 524-2955   18 holes, Par 72, Public
Opened: 1966   *Architect:* Don Cottle

Greens Fee: $19.50 with cart. Walking allowed weekdays
                    only.

Yardage: Blue tees — 6,495
                    Women's tees — 5,208
Course Rating: Blues — 69.9
                    Women's — 68.1

DOUBLEGATE COUNTRY CLUB

Albany (912) 436-6501   18 holes, Par 72, Private
Opened: 1964   *Architect:* Redesign by John LaFoy

Yardage: Championship tees — 7,000
                    Blue tees — 6,399
                    Women's tees — 5,830

Course Rating:	Championship — 72.1
	Blues — 69.2
	Women's — 66.8

DOUGLAS GOLF & COUNTRY CLUB

Douglas (912) 384-4707   18 holes, Par 72, Private
Opened: 1930   *Architect:* Don Cottle Jr.;
     members redesign 1989

Yardage:	Championship tees — 6,646
	Blue tees — 6,123
	Women's tees — 5,473
Course Rating:	Championship — 71.7
	Blues — 69.3
	Women's — 71.4

EVANS HEIGHTS GOLF COURSE

Claxton (912) 739-3003   18 holes, Par 72, Semi-Private
Opened: 1964   *Architect:* Don Cottle Jr.

Greens Fee: $20 with cart. Walking allowed.

Yardage:	Blue tees — 6,700
	Women's tees — 4,800
Course Rating:	Not yet rated

FARGO GOLF CLUB

Fargo (912) 637-5261   9 holes, Par 73, Public
Opened: 1961   *Architect:* Unknown

Greens Fee: $20 with cart. Walking allowed.

Yardage:	Blue tees — 3,087
	Women' tees — 2,307
Course Rating:	Blues — 69.6
	Women's — 66.1

FITZGERALD COUNTRY CLUB

Fitzgerald (912) 423-3560
Opened: 1932

9 holes, Par 71, Private
Architect: Unknown

Yardage: Blue tees — 6,001
                   Women's tees — 4,740
Course Rating: Blues — 67.6
                   Women's — 65.6

FOLKSTON GOLF CLUB

Folkston (912) 496-7155
Opened: 1958

18 holes, Par 72, Public
Architect: Ed Mattson

Greens fee: $15 daily with cart; $20 weekends, holidays.
                   Walking allowed.

Yardage: Blue tees — 6,268
                   Women's tees — 5,260
Course Rating: Blues — 69.5
                   Women's — 70.9

FOREST HEIGHTS COUNTRY CLUB

Statesboro (912) 764-3084
Opened: 1947

18 holes, Par 72, Private
Architect: George Cobb

Yardage: Blue tees — 6,848
                   Women's tees — 5,323
Course Rating: Blues — 72.9
                   Women's — 71.9

FORT STEWART GOLF COURSE

Ft. Stewart (912) 767-2370
Opened: 1963

18 holes, Par 72, Military
Architect: Military

Yardage: Blue tees — 6,305
                   Women's tees — 4,774

| Course Rating: | Blues — 68.4 |
| | Women's — 67.3 |

FOXFIRE GOLF CLUB

Vidalia (912) 538-8670   18 holes, Par 72, Semi-Private
Opened: 1992   *Architect:* Jim Bivins

Greens fee:	$21 with cart daily; $24 weekends, holidays. Walking allowed weekdays and after 1 p.m. weekends, holidays.
Yardage:	Championship tees — 6,726
	Blue tees — 6,218
	Women's tees — 4,757
Course Rating:	Not yet rated

FRANCIS LAKE GOLF COURSE

Lake Park (912) 559-7961   18 holes, Par 72, Semi-Private
Opened: 1972   *Architect:* Willard Byrd

Greens Fee:	$18 with cart daily; $21 weekends, holidays. Walking allowed after 3 p.m.
Yardage:	Blue tees — 6,700
	Women's tees — 5,500
Course Rating:	Blues — 71.0
	Women's — 70.1

GEORGIA VETERANS COURSE

Cordele (912) 276-2337   18 holes, Par 72, Public
Opened: 1990   *Architect:* Denis Griffiths

Green Fees:	$29 with cart. Walking allowed.
Yardage:	Blue tees — 7,008
	Women's tees — 5,180
Course Rating:	Blues — 73.1
	Women's — 73.5

GLYNCO GOLF CLUB

Brunswick (912) 264-9521   9 holes, Par 36, Public
Opened: 1967   *Architect:* Unknown

Greens Fee:	$20 with cart. Walking allowed.
Yardage:	Blue tees — 3,300
	Women's tees — 2,838
Course Rating:	Blues — 70.1
	Women's — 72.0

GREEN ACRES GOLF CLUB

Dexter (912) 875-3110   9 holes, Par 72, Private
Opened: 1968   *Architect:* Unknown

Yardage:	Championship tees — 6,800
	Blue tees — 6,600
	Women's tees — 5,200
Course Rating:	Championship — Not rated
	Blues — 67.4
	Women's — 67.4

THE HAMPTON CLUB

St. Simons Island (912) 634-0255   18 holes, Par 72, Semi-Private
Opened: 1989   *Architect:* Joe Lee

Greens Fee:	$64 with cart. Walking allowed after 3 p.m. for members only.
Yardage:	Blue tees — 6,465
	Women's tees — 5,233
Course Rating:	Blues — 71.4
	Women's — 69.9

Comment: Joe Lee has designed many courses in the state, and some people believe this is his best and surely most scenic. It's built along the marsh on the north end of the island, and it comes into play especially on Nos. 12-15. The ninth is only a par 4, but a lake can come into play three times.

HUNTER GOLF CLUB

Savannah (912) 352-5622   18 holes, Par 72, Private
Opened: 1964   *Architect:* Unknown

Yardage:	Blue tees — 6,565
	Women's tees — 5,488
Course Rating:	Blues — 72.1
	Women's — Not rated

JEFF DAVIS GOLF & COUNTRY CLUB

Hazelhurst (912) 375-5545   9 holes, Par 36, Private
Opened: 1965   *Architect:* Unknown

Yardage:	Blue tees — 3,636
	Women's tees — 2,592
Course Rating:	Blues — 72.5
	Women's — 69.3

JEKYLL ISLAND

Jekyll Island, once a playground for the rich and famous, is now a playground for the masses. It is state-owned, administered by the Jekyll Island Authority, and golfers from all 50 states have teed it up here at one time or another.

Getting there is about as easy as getting to Florida. You just take Exit 8 off 1-95 South, about an hour south of Savannah, and follow the signs. You can't miss it.

The island was bought in the 1950s from the nation's wealthiest and most powerful families — the Astors, Vanderbilts, Morgans, Pulitzers, Rockefellers and other deep pockets of their time — who once used the island as their winter vacation retreat.

It's a vacation paradise where golf is the main attraction. No matter your level of ability, there is a course here to satisfy the ego. Among the 63 holes is the Oceanside nine, the original course the millionaires built in the late 1800s. Although records are unclear, it is believed this nine was designed by the Scotsman Willie Dunn, runner-up in the first U.S. Open Championship in 1895.

In the late 1920s, the course was remodeled by the legendary Walter Travis, a contemporary of Ted Ray and Harry Vardon. Travis, an American, was the first foreigner to win the British Amateur. This win in 1903 caused quite a stir because he used his center-shafted Schenecktady putter.

Some of the holes on Oceanside have seen continuous play since early in the century. As an authentic links course, Oceanside was built on the natural undulations of Jekyll's dunes. Though barely over 3,000 yards, the sea breezes can make it play much longer. But at any distance, it's a pleasure.

In 1964, the Dick Wilson-designed Oleander was opened. This course cuts through the woods, marshes and palmettos and requires finesse and concentration. Wilson also created Pine Lakes, which opened in 1968. This course has mounded fairways, bunkers that guard the greens, and dogleg fairways that turn right and left — all marks of a Wilson layout.

Joe Lee, designer of Doral's Blue Monster, carved the 18-hole Indian Mounds from pine trees and marsh. It opened in 1975.

These are among the finest and most affordable public courses in the South. The courses handle about 200,000 rounds a year, and one nice feature is that the ninth hole of each course is close to the clubhouse.

JEKYLL ISLAND GOLF CLUB

Jekyll Island (912) 635-2368   63 holes, Resort

Green Fees: $35.70 with cart, April 15-Feb. 15; $37.80
Feb. 16-April 14. Walking allowed except for
one course designated as ride only.

SEASIDE (Original nine)
Opened: 1889, redesign 1920   *Architects:* Willie Dunn/Walter Travis

Yardage: Blue tees — 3,289
Women's tees — 2,570
Course Rating: Blues — 70.9
Women's 70.3

OLEANDER
Opened: 1964   *Architect:* Dick Wilson
Yardage: Blue tees — 6,679
Women's tees — 5,654
Course Rating: Blues — 72.0
Women's — 72.6

PINE LAKES
Opened: 1965   *Architect:* Dick Wilson

Yardage: Blue tees — 6,802
Women's tees — 5,742
Course Rating: Blues — 71.9
Women's — 71.9

INDIAN MOUNDS
Opened: 1977   *Architect:* Joe Lee

Yardage: Blue tees — 6,596
Women's tees — 5,349
Course Rating: Blues — 71.1
Women's — 70.0

Oleander is Jekyll Island's most demanding.

JOHNSON COUNTY COUNTRY CLUB

Wrightsville (912) 864-3301   9 holes, Par 36, Private
Opened: 1965   *Architect:* Unknown

Yardage:	Blue tees — 3,133
Course Rating:	Women's tees — 2,515
	Blues — 68.8
	Women's — 67.9

KINGS BAY GOLF CLUB

Kings Bay (912) 673-8476   18 holes, Par 72, Military
Opened: 1991   *Architect:* Arthur Hills

Yardage:	Blue tees — 6,586
Course Rating:	Women's tees — 5,278
	Blues — 71.5
	Women's — 70.4

LAKEVIEW GOLF CLUB

Blackshear (912) 449-4411   18 holes, Par 72, Semi-Private
Opened: 1969   *Architect:* Southern Engineers

Greens fee: $23 with cart. Walking allowed.

Yardage: Blue tees — 6,505
                  Women's tees — 4,928
Course Rating: Blues — 70.9
                  Women's — Not rated

THE LANDINGS

Because it's private and so very exclusive, the Landings at Skidaway Island is like an island unto itself. But those who've been privileged to wander inside the guard house gates will find some of the best golf courses ever constructed inside a residential community. Not one or two, but would you believe, six? And work may soon begin on number seven.

Nestled among the barrier islands near Savannah, the Landings is 20 years old, and in that time has brought in some of golf's most repsected designers to create their playground: Arnold Palmer, Arthur Hills, Williard Byrd and Tom Fazio. Ownership of even a lot in the Landings includes membership to the courses.

And what courses they are. The two Palmer designs, Marshwood and Magnolia, are inland-oriented and playable for all handicaps. Hills' Palmetto and Oakridge are the scenic kind, playing along lagoons and marshlands.

Byrd's Plantation course is shorter and tighter, but lacks nothing in the area of challenge or beauty.

The newest and perhaps best of the bunch is Fazio's Deer Creek, which uses both marsh and tall stands of mature oaks and pines to befuddle and bewitch its patrons.

THE LANDINGS

Skidaway Island (912) 598-2551   108 holes, Private

DEER CREEK

Opened: 1991   *Architect:* Tom Fazio

Yardage: Championship tees — 6,956
                     Blue tees — 6,527
                     Women's tees — 5,410

Course Rating: Championship — 73.4
                     Blues — 71.4
                     Women's — 71.0

PALMETTO

Opened: 1985   *Architect:* Arthur Hills

Yardage: Championship tees — 6,992
                     Blue tees — 6,457
                     Women's tees — 5,287

Course Rating: Championship — 74.7
                     Blues — 72.2
                     Women's — 71.3

PLANTATION

Opened: 1982   *Architect:* Williard Byrd

Yardage: Championship tees — 6,814
                     Blue tees — 6,230
                     Women's tees — 5,226

Course Rating: Championship — 73.4
                     Blues — 70.7
                     Women's — 70.8

MARSHWOOD

Opened: 1974   *Architect:* Arnold Palmer

Yardage: Championship — 6,762
                     Blue tees — 6,253
                     Women's tees — 5,361

Course Rating:	Championship — 73.2
	Blues — 71.2
	Women's — 71.0

MAGNOLIA

Opened: Front nine, 1977;   *Architects:* Ed Seay/Arnold Palmer
   Back nine, 1979

Yardage:	Championship tees — 6,741
	Blue tees — 6,260
	Women's tees — 5,185
Course Rating:	Championship — 73.9
	Blues — 71.7
	Women's — 70.7

OAKRIDGE

Opened: 1988   *Architect:* Arthur Hills

Yardage:	Championship tees — 6,675
	Blue tees — 6,207
	Women's tees — 5,002
Course Rating:	Championship — 73.1
	Blues — 71.3
	Women — 69.0

LAVIDA COUNTRY CLUB

Savannah (912) 925-2440   9 holes, Par 72, Private
Opened: 1962   *Architect:* George Cobb

Yardage:	Blue tees — 6,473
	Women's tees — 5,243
Course Rating:	Blues — 71.4
	Women's — 68.5

MALLARD POINT GOLF CLUB

Rochelle (912) 365-7810   18 holes, Par 72, Public
Opened: 1991   *Architects:* Steve McIntyre/Cliff Cagle/
Bruce Barrett

Greens fee: $18.50 with cart daily; $22.50 weekends, holidays. Walking allowed.

Yardage: Blue tees — 6,432
Women's tees — 4,882

Course Rating: Not rated

MARY CALDER GOLF CLUB

Savannah (912) 238-7100   9 holes, Par 35, Semi-Private
Opened: 1937   *Architect:* Unknown

Greens fee: $14.50 with cart daily; $16.50 weekends, holidays. Walking allowed.

Yardage: Blue tees — 3,000
Women's tees — 3,000

Course Rating: Blues — 68.8
Women's — 68.9

M.C.L.B. GOLF COURSE

Albany (912) 439-5211   9 holes, Par 72, Military
Opened: 1946   *Architect:* Military

Yardage: Blue tees — 6,252
Women's tees — 5,560

Course Rating: Blues — 69.8
Women's — 72.2

MAGNOLIA COUNTRY CLUB

Millen (912) 982-5717   9 holes, Par 70, Private
Opened: 1963   *Architect:* George Gunn

Yardage:	Blue tees — 5,570
Course Rating:	Blues — 66.0

McKENZIE MEMORIAL GOLF CLUB

Montezuma (912) 472-6126   9 holes, Par 70, Private
Opened: 1931   *Architect:* Sid Clark

Yardage:	Blue tees — 5,736
	Women's tees — 5,054
Course Rating:	Blue — 67.5
	Women's — 67.5

MEADOW LAKES GOLF CLUB

Statesboro (912) 839-3191   18 holes, Par 73, Public
Opened: 1985   *Architect:* Arthur Davis

Greens fee:	20 with cart; Walking allowed weekdays only.
Yardage:	Blue tees — 6,432
	Women's tees — 5,339
Course Rating:	Blues — 71.8
	Women's — 68.6

NORTHLAKE GOLF & COUNTRY CLUB

Valdosta (912) 247-8986   18 holes, Par 68, Public
Opened: 1985   *Architect:* Several

Greens fee:	$16 with cart daily; $19 weekends, holidays. Walking allowed.
Yardage:	Blue tees — 5,193 Women's tees — 4,700
Course Rating:	Blues — 67.0 Women's — 67.0

OCILLA COUNTRY CLUB

Ocilla (912) 468-7512   9 holes, Par 72, Private
Opened: 1936   *Architect:* Unknown

Yardage:	Blue tees — 3,236 Women's tees — 2,498
Course Rating:	Blues — 70.6 Women's — 68.2

OKEFENOKEE COUNTRY CLUB

Blackshear (912) 283-7235   18 holes, Par 72, Private
Opened: 1923   *Architect:* Joe Lee

Yardage:	Blue tees — 6,784 Women's tees — 5,063
Course Rating:	Blues — 71.3 Women's — 69.1

OSPREY COVE GOLF AND COUNTRY CLUB

St. Mary's (912) 882-5575   18 holes, Par 72, Semi-private
Opened: *Architect:* Mark McCumber

Green Fees:	$38 daily with cart. $43 weekends and holidays. Walking allowed at non-peak times.

Yardage:	Championship tees — 6,791
	Blue tees — 6,269
	Women's tees — 5,263
Course Rating:	Championship — 74.1
	Blues — 73.0
	Women's — 71.1

Comment: This could be one of the state's best kept secrets. Located just off Exit 1 on I-95 South, this Mark McCumber-designed course overlooks natural salt marshes and wood-lands. It's a challenge from the back tees, but enjoyable no matter where you tee it up. The 9th and 18th holes play to a common green.

PACHITLA CREEK GOLF CLUB

Edison (912) 835-2300   9 holes, Par 36, Semi-Private
Opened: 1992   *Architect:* Andy Stephens

Greens fee:	$15 with cart daily; $17 weekends, holidays. Walking allowed.
Yardage:	Blue tees — 3,102
	Women's tees — 2,152
Course Rating:	Not yet rated

PINE BLUFF COUNTRY CLUB

Eastman (912) 374-0991   18 holes, Par 72, Semi-Private
Opened: 1992   *Architect:* Members

Greens fee:	$14.50 with cart daily; $17.50 weekends, holidays. Walking allowed.
Yardage:	Blue tees — 6,500
	Women's tees — 4,700
Course Rating:	Not yet rated

PINE FOREST COUNTRY CLUB

Jesup (912) 427-6505   18 holes, Par 72, Private
Opened: 1970   *Architect:* Unknown

Yardage:	Blue tees — 6,496	
	Women's tees — 5,396	
Course Rating:	Blues — 69.4	
	Women's — 70.1	

PINE HILLS GOLF CLUB

Winder (706) 867-3150   18 holes, Par 72, Public
Opened: 1960   *Architect:* Unknown

Greens fee:	$17 with cart daily; $23 weekends, holidays. Walking allowed non-peak times.
Yardage:	Blue tees — 6,423
	Women's tees — 4,982
Course Rating:	Blues — 70.0
	Women's — 68.7

Comment: Anyone who's driven to Athens on Highway 29 has seen this course just outside Winder. It's not difficult and it's well maintained. Pine Hills is a good place for a dad to take his son and introduce him to the the game.

PINE ISLAND CLUB

Tifton (912) 387-7600   9 holes, Par 27, Public
Opened: 1990   *Architect:* Paul Massey

Greens fee:	$14 with cart. Walking allowed.
Yardage:	Blue tees — 1,363
	Women's tees — 983
Course Rating:	Not rated

PINECREST COUNTRY CLUB

Pelham (912) 294-8525   9 holes, Par 72, Private
Opened: 1943   *Architect:* Unknown

Yardage: Blue tees — 6,850
                    Women's tees — 6,513
Course Rating: Not rated

PINEKNOLL COUNTRY CLUB

Sylvester (912) 776-3455   9 holes, Par 72, Private
Opened: 1966   *Architect:* Bill Amick

Yardage: Blue tees — 6,472
                    Women's tees — 6,436
Course Rating: Blues — 70.0
                    Women's — 71.0

QUITMAN COUNTRY CLUB

Quitman (912) 263-4942   9 holes, Par 76, Private
Opened: 1913   *Architect:* Unknown

Yardage: Blue tees — 5,290
Course Rating: Blues — 68.5

RADIUM COUNTRY CLUB

Albany (912) 883-2685   18 holes, Par 72, Private
Opened: 1927   *Architect:* John Law Kerr

Yardage: Blue tees — 6,434
                    Women's tees — 5,441
Course Rating: Blues — 70.1
                    Women's — 75.0

RANDOLPH COUNTRY CLUB

Cuthbert (912) 732-2351   9 holes, Par 70, Private
Opened: 1932   *Architect:* Unknown

Yardage:	Blue tees — 6,102
	Women's tees — 6,002
Course Rating:	Not rated

ST. SIMONS ISLAND CLUB

St. Simons Island (912) 638-5130   18 holes, Par 72, Public
Opened: 1976   *Architect:* Joe Lee

Greens fee:	$54 with cart. Walking allowed after 3 p.m.
Yardage:	Blue tees — 6,490
	Women's tees — 5,361
Course Rating:	Blues — 71.8
	Women's — 70.0

Comment: This course is included in Sea Island's Cloister package. It's tight and tree-lined in places, open and at the mercy of the elements in others.

SAVANNAH GOLF CLUB

A case can be made that Savannah has bragging rights to being the first city in the U.S. where golf was played, as early as 1795. The evidence comes from an article in the September 1796 issue of the Georgia Gazette announcing an anniversary meeting of the Savannah Golf Club for the purpose of electing officers.

There is no record, however, of where the game of golf may have been played in Savannah.

The Savannah Golf Club, as we now know it, was incorporated in December 1899 and opened its nine holes in early 1900. It was 2,945 yards, and par, which was then called bogey, was 39.

Each hole had a name. Number three, for instance, was "Hell," 388 yards, par 5, where the approach shot was described thusly: "You have a large bunker to carry on your second, and a ditch on each side, and if you foozle your second, Hell, the hole is properly named."

Number seven, 502 yards, was properly dubbed "Far Way." And the 300-yard ninth was simply "Home Again."

The Savannah Golf Club also has a rich tournament history. It was the host club for five State Amateurs and will be again in 1994. The legendary Watts Gunn of East Lake won it there in 1927; former Georgia Tech great Dynamite Goodloe took the title in 1954; and Atlanta's Charlie Harrison, then 28, won in 1959, the last year the tournament was played at match play.

The club's alumni rolls also are impressive. At one time, it claimed two USGA champions — Cecile Maclaurin, the 1976 Senior Women's Amateur, and Hollis Stacy, the 1977 U.S. Women's Open. Stacy won the title again in 1978 and '84. She also won consecutive U.S. Girls Junior titles, '69, '70 and '71. Gene Sauers, who has won twice on the PGA Tour, has also been a member.

THE SAVANNAH GOLF CLUB

Savannah (912) 232-2156   18 holes, Par 72, Private
Opened: 1794   *Architect:* Unknown

Yardage: Blue tees — 6,338
         Women's tees — 5,409
Course Rating: Blues — 70.0
         Women's — 70.6

SEA ISLAND GOLF CLUB

Golf at Sea Island. It doesn't get any better than this. Majestic oaks and pines recall the grandeur of antebellum Retreat Plantation to make every hole of the four distinctive nines a perfect golfing experience.

The Plantation Nine was first to open in 1927, followed by Seaside in 1929, Retreat in 1960 and Marshside in 1974. Mix and match them for an 18-hole layout and it's all the golf course you want.

Depending on the winds, Seaside can be as docile as an old dog laying in front of a roaring fire, or as hostile as a pit bull. The legendary Bobby Jones played it first in the mid 1930s and proclaimed it as one of the best nines he'd ever seen. LPGA Hall-of-Famer Betsy Wright still proclaims it as her favorite golf course.

Seaside is the best nine and offers a new personality each day. The first, second and fourth are relatively easy par 4s one day, but when the wind shifts and comes from the south, you'll take your five with a smile.

Anyone who's played Seaside will tell you that the 424-yard par 4 seventh is one of the best holes anywhere. It's the most intimidating tee shot on the course, demanding a 220-yard carry of White Heron Creek. Bailing out right leaves you with a daunting second over a two-story high bunker that hides the green.

Sea Island has played host to the State Amateur three times — in 1931, 1939 and 1989 — and an Atlanta Yates has won each of them. After Charlie won in 1931, his brother Dan commented on the eve of the 1938 event, "I'd like to win this where by brother won it," and he did so, defeating Sonny Swift 1-up with a birdie on the 37th hole.

In 1989, Danny Yates III admitted to "feeling a lot of pressure," before the first round. But he came through in typical Yates fashion with an opening 66 on the way to victory, 50 years after his father.

The seventh at Sea Island's Seaside is scary.

SEA ISLAND GOLF CLUB

St. Simons (912) 638-5118   36 holes, All par 72, Resort

Greens Fee: $89 w/ cart. No transient play from March–April. Walking okay, but caddies required.

RETREAT
Opened: 1960   *Architect:* Dick Wilson

Yardage: Championship tees — 3,326
Blue tees — 2,760
Women's tees — 2,617

SEASIDE
Opened: 1929   *Architects:* Colt/Allison

Yardage: Championship tees — 3,384
Blue tees — 2,822
Women's tees — 2,569

PLANTATION
Opened: 1927   *Architects:* Walter Travis; Colt and Allison
redesign in 1929; Rees Jones redesign in 1992

Yardage: Championship tees — 3,516
Blue tees — 3,019
Women's tees — 2,609

MARSHSIDE
Opened: 1973   *Architect:* Joe Lee

Yardage: Championship tees — 3,192
Blue tees — 2,549
Women's tees — 2,439

SEASIDE/RETREAT
Course Ratings: Championship — 72.6
Blues — 68.6
Women's — 70.1

PLANTATION/MARSH:
Course Ratings: Championship — 71.9
                        Blues — 68.0
                        Women's — 68.5

SEASIDE/PLANTATION
Course Ratings: Championship — 73.2
                        Blues — 69.5
                        Women's — 69.1

RETREAT/MARSHSIDE
Course Ratings: Championship — 71.2
                        Blues — 66.5
                        Women's — 69.5

MARSHSIDE/SEASIDE
Course Ratings: Championship — 71.3
                        Blues — 66.4
                        Women's — 69.4

RETREAT/PLANTATION
Course Ratings: Championship — 72.8
                        Blues — 69.5
                        Women's — 69.3

SEA PALMS GOLF & TENNIS CLUB

St. Simons (912) 638-3351   27 holes, Par 72, Public
Opened: Tall Pines/Great Oaks, 1967;   *Architect:* Tall Pines/Great
Sea Palms West, 1975   Oaks, George Cobb;
                       Sea Palms West, Tom Jackson

Greens fee: $53 with cart. No walking.

TALL PINES/GREAT OAKS
Yardage: Blue tees — 6,658
                        Women's tees — 5,328
Course Rating: Blues — 72.1
                        Women's — 70.9

GREAT OAKS/SEA PALMS WEST
Yardage: Blue tees — 6,350
                     Women's tees — 5,113
Course Rating: Blues — 70.6
                     Women's — 69.3

SEA PALMS WEST/TALL PINES
Yardage: Blue tees — 6,198
                     Women's tees — 5,249
Course Rating: Blues — 69.7
                     Women's — 70.4

Comment: Though Sea Palms is dwarfed in history and reputation by Sea Pines, it more than holds its own with the golfing public that demands well-conditioned courses that are neither too demanding nor push-overs. There's a lot of diversity here. Though Tall Pines and Great Oaks are considered the more formidable nines, the shorter West course — at less than 3,000 yards — is more difficult due to the ocean winds.

SHERATON-SAVANNAH RESORT

Wilmington Island (912) 897-1612   18 holes, Par 72, Resort
Opened: 1927   *Architects:* Donald Ross/Willard Byrd

Greens Fee: $48.10 w/ cart. No walking.

Yardage: Championship tees — 6,876
                     Blue tees — 6,528
                     Women's tees — 5,328
Course Rating: Championship — 73.5
                     Blues — 71.6
                     Women's — 70.6

Comment: Built in 1926 and opened as the General Oglethorpe Inn, this stately facility has undergone several facelifts and another is expected. The course was designed in 1927 and re-designed by Willard Byrd in '66. Much of Ross's work is still evident, however. It's a course you could play every day and never tire of. The 395-yard par 4 15th is one of Georgia's best

18. The State Amateur has been held here twice, won by Allen Doyle in 1979 and Peter Persons in '84. It's also the home of the Georgia Michelob Open, which has produced such winners as the PGA Tour's Larry Nelson and Gene Sauers and the Senior Tour's DeWitt Weaver.

The demanding fifth green at Sheraton Savannah

SOUTHBRIDGE GOLF CLUB

Savannah (912) 651-5455   18 holes, Par 72, Public
Opened: 1989   *Architect:* Rees Jones

Green Fees:	$29 daily with cart; $35 weekends, holidays. Walking allowed weekdays and after 2 p.m. weekends and holidays.
Yardage:	Championship tees — 6,990 Blue tees — 6,458 Women's tees — 5,181
Course Rating:	Championship — 73.4 Blues — 71.4 Women's — 69.2

Comment: The mark of a good course is being able to remember every hole two days after you play it for the first time. Southbridge has that distinction. Every hole is different. From the back tees, it's all the low handicapper can handle, but from the blues the average player can handle it. Southbridge may have the best four par 3s of any daily fee course in Georgia. Easy to get to, less than 10 minutes off I-95 on I-16 East.

SPRING HILL COUNTRY CLUB

Tifton (912) 382-6745   18 holes, Par 72, Private
Opened: 1965   *Architect:* Ozie Jones

Yardage: Championship tees — 6,980
                    Blue tees — 6,420
                    Women's tees — 5,200
Course Rating: Championship — 72.0
                    Blue — 70.0
                    Women's — 74.0

STONE CREEK GOLF COURSE

Valdosta (912) 247-2527   18 holes, Par 72, Semi-Private
Opened: 1992   *Architect:* Jeff Burton

Greens fee: $29 with cart daily; $34 weekends, holidays.
                    Walking allowed weekdays and after 1 p.m.
                    weekends, holidays.

Yardage: Blue tees — 6,177
                    Women's tees — 4,219
Course Rating: Blues — 68.9
                    Women's — 64.4

Comment: It's not long, but it is testy. The fairways are narrow and undulating, and water forces quite a few lay-up shots. The par 5 third hole plays over a large beaver pond.

SUNSET COUNTRY CLUB

Moultrie (912) 890-5555   18 holes, Par 72, Private
Opened: 1953   *Architect:* Emory Lee

Yardage: Blue tees — 6,846
                       Women's tees — 5,344
Course Rating: Blues — 71.9
                       Women's — 70.0

SUNSWEET HILLS GOLF CLUB

Tifton (912) 382-0011   18 holes, Par 72, Public
Opened: 1992   *Architect:* Don McMillan

Greens fee: $23 with cart daily; $28 weekends, holidays.
                       Walking allowed.

Yardage: Championship tees — 6,800
                       Blue tees — 6,400
                       Women's tees — 5,300
Course Rating: Championship — 71.5
                       Blues — 71.2
                       Women's — 69.9

Comment: Sunsweet Hills gives you two different looks. The front nine is cut through a pecan orchard and will test your accuracy. The back is hilly with elevated landing areas. Water comes into play on six holes; the par 3 11th drops 40 feet over some scrub oaks; and one of the par fives has a five-plateau green. If you're a good iron player, you'll love it here.

SWAINSBORO GOLF & COUNTRY CLUB

Swainsboro (912) 237-6116   9 holes, Par 72, Public
Opened: 1953   *Architect:* Unknown

Greens fee: $16 with cart. Walking allowed.

Yardage: Blue tees — 6,107
                  Women's tees — 4,978
Course Rating: Blues — 69.0
                  Women's — 65.7

TOWN AND COUNTRY CLUB

Blakely (912) 723-4700   9 holes, Par 72, Private
Opened: 1954   *Architect:* Members

Yardage: Blue tees — 6,176
                  Women's tees — 5,724
Course Rating: Blues — 68.2
                  Women's — Not rated

TOWN CREEK COUNTRY CLUB

Hawkinsville (912) 783-0128   9 holes, Par 70, Semi-Private
Opened: 1956   *Architect:* Members

Yardage: Blue tees — 6,170
                  Women's tees — 4,778
Course Rating: Blues — 67.5
                  Women's — 65.5

TURNER GOLF COURSE

Albany (912) 430-5267   18 holes, Par 71, Public
Opened: 1957   *Architect:* Military

Greens fee: $16.80 with cart daily; $21.80 weekends,
                  holidays. Walking allowed.

Yardage:	Blue tees — 6,014
	Women's tees — 5,122
Course Rating:	Blues — 69.4
	Women's (Par 73) — 70.0

TWIN CITY COUNTRY CLUB

Sandersville (912) 552-7894   18 holes, Par 72, Private
Opened: 1928   *Architect:* Unknown

Yardage:	Blue tees — 6,436
	Women's tees — 5,309
Course Rating:	Blues — 70.6
	Women's — 70.7

VALDOSTA COUNTRY CLUB

Valdosta (912) 241-2000   27 holes, Par 72, Private
Opened: Plantation/Bottom, 1976   *Architect:* Joe Lee
          Belle Meade, 1987

PLANTATION/BOTTOM
Yardage:	Blue tees — 6,739
	Women's tees — 5,113
Course Rating:	Blues — 71.3
	Women's — 69.5

BOTTOM/BELLE MEADE
Yardage:	Blue tees — 6,710
	Women's tees — 5,332
Course Rating:	Blues — 71.4
	Women's — 69.7

BELLE MEADE/PLANTATION
Yardage:	Blue tees — 6,699
	Women's tees — 5,115
Course Rating:	Blues — 71.3
	Women's — 70.3

VIDALIA COUNTRY CLUB

Vidalia (912) 537-3531   18 holes, Par 72   Private
Opened: 1969   *Architect:* Unknown

Yardage:	Blue tees — 6,451
	Women's tees — 5,084
Course Rating:	Blues — 70.3
	Women's — 67.5

Wallace Adams at Little Ocmulgee State Park

WALLACE ADAMS GOLF COURSE

McRae (912) 868-6651   18 holes, Par 72, Public
Opened: 1965   *Architect:* Unknown

Greens fee:	$29 with cart. Walking allowed.
Yardage:	Blue tees — 6,625
	Women's tees — 5,001
Course Rating:	Blues — 70.8
	Women's — 67.5

WANEE LAKE GOLF CLUB

Ashburn (912) 567-2727   9 holes, Par 72, Semi-Private
Opened: 1969   *Architect:* Unknown

Greens fee: $20 with cart daily; $22 weekends, holidays.
                     Walking allowed weekdays only.

Yardage: Blue tees — 6,244
                     Women's tees — 5,222
Course Rating: Blues — 69.3
                     Women's — 69.1

WILLOW LAKE GOLF CLUB

Metter (912) 685-2724   18 holes, Par 72, Semi-Private
Opened: 1964   *Architect:* Arthur Davis

Greens fee: $21 with cart. Walking allowed.

Yardage: Blue tees — 6,401
                     Women's tees — 4,864
Course Rating: Blues — 70.5
                     Women's — 68.0

WILLOWPEG GOLF CLUB

Rincon (912) 826-2092   18 holes, Par 72, Semi-Private
Opened: 1989   *Architect:* Ward Northrup

Greens fee: $26 with cart daily; $29 weekends, holidays.
                     Walking allowed for members.

Yardage: Blue tees — 6,575
                     Women's tees — 5,480
Course Rating: Blues — 70.5
                     Women's — 70.8

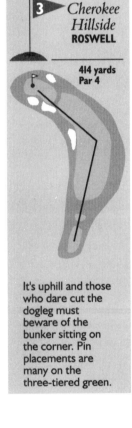

3 *Cherokee Hillside*
ROSWELL

414 yards
Par 4

It's uphill and those who dare cut the dogleg must beware of the bunker sitting on the corner. Pin placements are many on the three-tiered green.

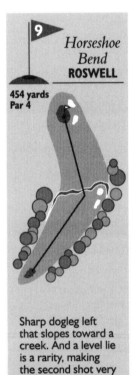

9 *Horseshoe Bend*
ROSWELL

454 yards
Par 4

Sharp dogleg left that slopes toward a creek. And a level lie is a rarity, making the second shot very difficult. A very difficult green to read from any angle.

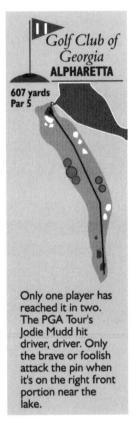

11 *Golf Club of Georgia*
ALPHARETTA

607 yards
Par 5

Only one player has reached it in two. The PGA Tour's Jodie Mudd hit driver, driver. Only the brave or foolish attack the pin when it's on the right front portion near the lake.

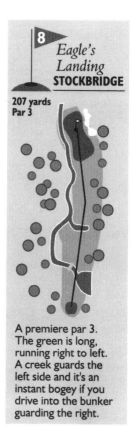

8

Eagle's Landing
STOCKBRIDGE

207 yards
Par 3

A premiere par 3. The green is long, running right to left. A creek guards the left side and it's an instant bogey if you drive into the bunker guarding the right.

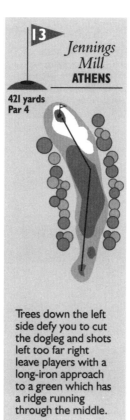

13

Jennings Mill
ATHENS

421 yards
Par 4

Trees down the left side defy you to cut the dogleg and shots left too far right leave players with a long-iron approach to a green which has a ridge running through the middle.

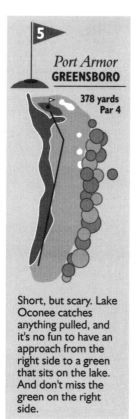

5

Port Armor
GREENSBORO

378 yards
Par 4

Short, but scary. Lake Oconee catches anything pulled, and it's no fun to have an approach from the right side to a green that sits on the lake. And don't miss the green on the right side.

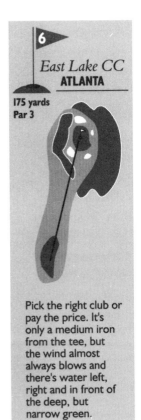

6

East Lake CC
ATLANTA

175 yards
Par 3

Pick the right club or pay the price. It's only a medium iron from the tee, but the wind almost always blows and there's water left, right and in front of the deep, but narrow green.

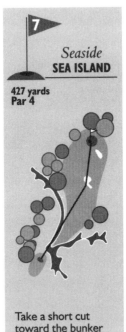

7

Seaside
SEA ISLAND

427 yards
Par 4

Take a short cut toward the bunker and you have a blind shot to the green. The best way is straight ahead, but a poor tee shot could wind up in the canal.

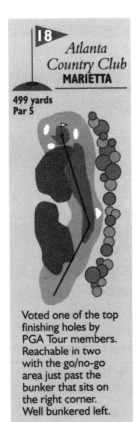

18

Atlanta Country Club
MARIETTA

499 yards
Par 5

Voted one of the top finishing holes by PGA Tour members. Reachable in two with the go/no-go area just past the bunker that sits on the right corner. Well bunkered left.

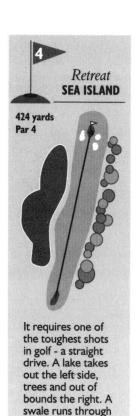

4

Retreat
SEA ISLAND

424 yards
Par 4

It requires one of the toughest shots in golf - a straight drive. A lake takes out the left side, trees and out of bounds the right. A swale runs through the green.

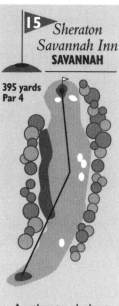

15 *Sheraton Savannah Inn*
SAVANNAH

395 yards
Par 4

Another tough short hole. Hard driving hole with water left, out of bounds right. Difficult approach to a green that is small, mounded and always hard and fast.

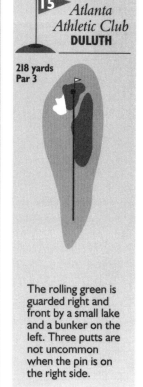

15 *Atlanta Athletic Club*
DULUTH

218 yards
Par 3

The rolling green is guarded right and front by a small lake and a bunker on the left. Three putts are not uncommon when the pin is on the right side.

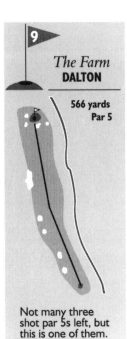

9

The Farm
DALTON

**566 yards
Par 5**

Not many three shot par 5s left, but this is one of them. Mounds and pot bunkers catch anything left and a stream guards the right. Narrow green is surrounded by bunkers.

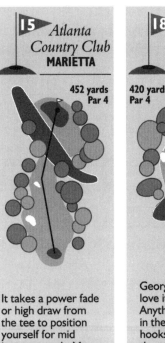
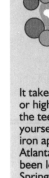

15 *Atlanta Country Club*
MARIETTA

**452 yards
Par 4**

It takes a power fade or high draw from the tee to position yourself for mid iron approach. Many Atlanta Classics have been lost here, Mike Springer in 1991 the most recent.

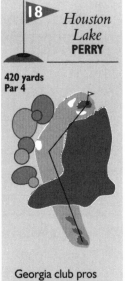

18 *Houston Lake*
PERRY

**420 yards
Par 4**

Georgia club pros love it and hate it. Anything hit right is in the water. Big hooks or pulls are in the woods, and there's no getting up and down if you miss the deep but narrow green.

12 *Augusta National* **AUGUSTA**

155 yards
Par 3

Amen Corner's hell hole. So inviting distance wise but so dangerous when the wind swirls through the pines, which it always seems to do, especially on Sunday when the leaders arrive.

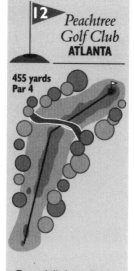

12 *Peachtree Golf Club* **ATLANTA**

455 yards
Par 4

Downhill through a chute of tall trees with a creek crossing the fairway near the landing area. Then it's uphill to an elevated green guarded by bunkers. Peachtree's best hole and most difficult.

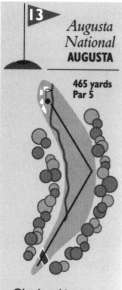

13 *Augusta National* **AUGUSTA**

465 yards
Par 5

Oh, that this was Augusta National's finishing hole. Imagine someone needing an eagle to win and having to hit a 3-iron off a sidehill lie with that devilish creek to cross.

INDEX